THE COMPLETE STEP-BY-STEP
COOKBOOK

THE COMPLETE STEP-BY-STEP
COOKBOOK

With more than 200 international recipes
for Seafood, Pasta, Meat, Vegetables and Desserts

Antonio Piccinardi · Savina Roggero

Webb & Bower

MICHAEL JOSEPH

Note: an asterisk after an ingredient refers to the Basic Recipes section at the end of the book, where instructions or information about the ingredient or its preparation are given.

First published in Great Britain 1989 by
Webb & Bower (Publishers) Limited
5 Cathedral Close, Exeter, Devon EX1 1EZ
in association with Michael Joseph Limited
27 Wright's Lane, London W8 5TZ

Published in association with the Penguin Group
Penguin Books Ltd, Registered Offices: Harmondsworth, Middlesex, England
Penguin Books Australia Ltd, Ringwood, Victoria, Australia
Penguin Books Canada Ltd, 2801 John Street, Markham, Ontario, Canada L3R 1D4
Penguin Books (NZ) Ltd, 182–190 Wairau Road, Auckland 10, New Zealand

Copyright © 1988 Arnoldo Mondadori Editore, S.p.A., Milan
English translation copyright © 1988 Arnoldo Mondadori Editore S.p.A., Milan

British Library Cataloguing in Publication Data
Piccinardi, Antonio
    The complete step-by-step cookbook.
    1. Food – Recipes
    I. Title   II. Roggero, Savina
    641.5

    ISBN 0–86350–311–X

Translated by Caroline Beamish, Elaine Hardy, Sara Harris

Typeset in Great Britain by Tradespools Ltd, Frome, Somerset
Printed and bound in Spain by Artes Graficas, Toledo
D. L. TO: 1215 -1989

Contents

Introduction

This collection of more than two hundred recipes consists of famous dishes from all over the world along with others that are creative, original and unique to this volume. There are elaborate recipes alongside others that take no time at all to prepare. All feature clear and detailed instructions, organised into step-by-step stages and often accompanied by a series of pictures illustrating the vital moments of preparation. All the recipes, therefore, from the simplest to the most complicated, are presented in a way that is easy to follow.

In the final chapter there is also an essential reference section – a selection of useful cooking tips ranging from advice on how to choose and cook certain foods, to basic recipes and suggestions on how to serve different dishes. This book can therefore be of practical use to everybody: the skilful and experienced cook will have the possibility to create wonderfully delicious and unusual menus; those less expert can equally aspire to the creation of imaginative dishes, guided by the illustrations and instructions accompanying the recipes.

Appetizers

Prawn cocktail

Preparation: 30 minutes
(+ 1 hour for chilling)

20 cooked Dublin Bay
prawns
salt
225 ml/8 fl oz mayonnaise
1¹/₂ tbsp ketchup
¹/₂ tsp Worcestershire sauce
2 tsp brandy
1 lettuce
parsley
1 lemon

1   Shell the prawns.

2   Mix together the mayonnaise, ketchup, Worcestershire sauce and brandy.

3   Wash and dry the lettuce and finely shred the white part.

4   Mix the prawns with the sauce, reserving a few for the garnish.

5   Distribute the lettuce between four stemmed glasses, lining each with a whole outer leaf.

6   Spoon the prawn cocktail into each glass and garnish with a slice of lemon and a little parsley. Chill for 1 hour before serving.

Salmon mousse

Preparation: 1 hour (+ 5
  hours for the mousse to
  set)

400 g/14 oz fresh salmon, in
  one piece
500 ml/18 fl oz *court-
  bouillon**
2 level tbsp powdered
  gelatine
3 tbsp dry sherry
2 tbsp lemon juice
salt and pepper
225 ml/8 fl oz double cream
3 egg whites
2 tbsp oil
gherkins
1 lemon

1   Place the salmon in a
casserole;pour in the *court-
bouillon*, cover with foil and
bake in a preheated oven at
180°C/350°F/mark 4 for 20
minutes.

2   Leave the salmon to
cool slightly. Remove and
discard the skin and bones.
Flake into pieces and place
in a blender or food
processor. Dissolve the
gelatine over gentle heat in
125 ml/4 fl oz of *court-
bouillon* and pour into the
blender.

3   Add the sherry, lemon
juice, and salt and pepper
and liquidize until smooth.

4   Whip the cream until
firm but not too stiff. Beat
the egg whites until stiff and
fold both into the salmon
mixture.

5   Brush the inside of a
large mould or individual
ramekins with oil, pour in
the mousse and chill in the
refrigerator for at least 5
hours.

6   Turn the mousse out on
to a serving dish and garnish
with sliced gherkins and
lemon.

Seafood salad

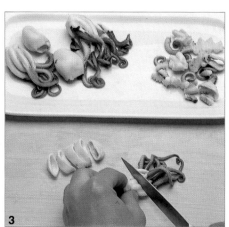

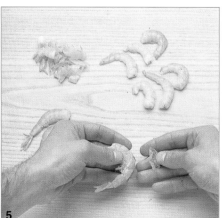

Preparation: 1 hour (+ 1
hour for cleaning mussels
and razor clams)

6 baby octopuses, squid or
cuttlefish, cleaned (total
weight 350 g/12 oz)
salt and pepper
1 celery stick
225 g/8 oz mussels
350 g/12 oz razor clams
1 clove garlic
350 g/12 oz prawns
1 bunch parsley
4 tbsp oil
$^1/_2$ lemon

1   Gently lower the baby
octopuses, tentacles first,
into boiling salted water.
Add the chopped celery and
cook for 8 minutes, then
drain.

2   Wash the mussels and
razor clams and leave under
running water for 1 hour.
Drain, place in a saucepan
and sprinkle with the
chopped garlic. Cover and
cook gently for 4 minutes
until the shells open.
Remove the meat from the
shells and place in a dish.

3   When the octopuses
have cooled, cut off the
tentacles and cut the bodies
into rings. Place in the dish
with the mussels and razor
clams.

4   Place the prawns, heads
removed, in a small
saucepan with a little water
and salt. Cover and cook for
4 minutes.

5   Peel the prawns and add
to the other seafood.

6   Rinse and dry the
parsley. Chop finely and
sprinkle over the mixed
seafood. Season with oil,
lemon juice, salt and
pepper. Stir well before
serving.

Salade niçoise

Preparation: 1 hour (+ 30
minutes for soaking the
anchovies)

50 g/2 oz tinned anchovies
salt
225 g/8 oz potatoes
225 g/8 oz green beans
2 hard-boiled eggs
225 g/8 oz tomatoes
1 lettuce
225 g/8 oz tinned tuna
4 tbsp oil
2 tbsp vinegar
50 g/2 oz small black olives

1   Drain the anchovies and
rinse under cold running
water; divide each one in
half, remove the backbone
and leave to soak for 30
minutes.

2   Boil the potatoes in their
skins in salted water for
approximately 20 minutes.
Leave to cool; peel and slice
thinly.

3   String the beans and boil
in salted water for about 8
minutes. Drain and leave to
cool.

4   Cut each egg into four
and slice the tomatoes.

5   Rinse and dry the lettuce
leaves and cut into shreds.
Drain the tuna and flake.

6   Prepare a vinaigrette by
beating together the oil,
vinegar and a little salt.

7   Place the lettuce, beans
and potatoes in a bowl and
dress with half the
vinaigrette. Toss well.

8   Arrange on a serving
platter and garnish with the
hard-boiled eggs, tomatoes,
anchovies and olives. Pour
over the remaining
vinaigrette.

Sardines in "saòr"

Preparation: 1 hour (+ 30 minutes for soaking the sultanas and 1 day for marinating the sardines)

800 g/1³⁄₄ lb fresh sardines
3 tbsp flour
oil for deep frying
2 large onions
salt
125 ml/4 fl oz white wine vinegar
1-2 tbsp sultanas
50 g/2 oz pine nuts
2 tbsp candied peel
125 ml/4 fl oz soured cream

1   Clean the sardines, remove the scales and rinse thoroughly.

2   Drain the sardines well and coat lightly with flour.

3   Fry the sardines in plenty of very hot oil.

4   When the sardines are golden brown and cooked, drain on kitchen paper.

5   Slice the onions finely, sprinkle with salt, and fry in the remaining oil. Add 125 ml/4 fl oz water and cook for 10 minutes. Pour in half the vinegar and simmer for a few minutes.

6   Place the sardines in a shallow dish, pour over the remaining vinegar, and sprinkle with the soaked and drained sultanas, pine nuts and chopped candied peel.

7   Sprinkle with the onions and soured cream. Cover and leave to stand in a cool place – not in the refrigerator – for 24 hours before serving.

Rollmops

Preparation: 1 hour (+ 4 hours for soaking and 3 days for marinating)

4 fresh herrings
125 g/4 oz salt
275 ml/10 fl oz white wine vinegar
2 bay leaves
8 black peppercorns
fresh dill
1 tsp mixed spices (coriander, juniper berries, dill)
2 onions
2 gherkins

1   Cut the head and tail from the herrings; open the fish flat and remove the bones and entrails.

2   Dissolve the salt in 500 ml/18 fl oz water in a bowl and leave the herrings to soak for at least 4 hours. Turn them every 30 minutes. Drain and dry the fillets.

3   Bring the vinegar to the boil in a saucepan. Add the bay leaf, peppercorns, fresh dill and spices, remove from the heat and leave to cool.

4   Slice one onion and the gherkins and wrap each fillet around a slice of onion and gherkin.

5   Place the rolled fillets in a glass or earthenware jar and place the remaining slices of onion and gherkin between them. Pour in the vinegar, cover and leave to marinate in a cool place for 3 to 4 days.

6   Slice the remaining onion and serve raw with the rollmops. Serve with slices of brown bread or rye bread and butter.

Soused herrings

Preparation: 40 minutes
(+ 12 hours for
marinating the herrings)

2 carrots
1 onion
275 ml/10 fl oz white wine
225 ml/8 fl oz wine vinegar
2 bay leaves
2 sprigs thyme
6 white peppercorns
3 cloves
salt
600 g/1¾ lb fresh herrings
1 tbsp chopped parsley

1   Prepare the marinade:
finely chop the carrots and
onion. Place in a saucepan
with the wine, wine vinegar,
1 bay leaf, 1 sprig thyme,
the peppercorns, cloves and
a pinch of salt. Bring to the
boil and simmer gently for
10 minutes.

2   Clean the herrings:
remove the scales,
backbone, heads and tails.
Wash and pat dry with
kitchen paper.

3   Place the herrings in a
flameproof casserole,
sprinkle with the chopped
parsley, 1 crumbled bay leaf
and a sprig of thyme.

4   Pour the marinade over
the herrings and cook over a
moderate heat for 5
minutes.

5   Allow to cool, cover and
refrigerate for 12 hours.

6   Remove from the
refrigerator at least 2 hours
before serving.

Herring salad

Preparation: 1 hour (+ 24 hours for marinating the herrings)

4 salted herrings
2 potatoes
2 beetroot
1 cooking apple
1 cucumber
125 g/4 oz cooked veal
¹/₂ onion
2 tbsp oil
2 tbsp wine vinegar
salt and pepper
3 hard-boiled eggs
¹/₂ tbsp mustard
3 tbsp soured cream or plain yoghurt
1 tbsp chopped dill

1   Soak the herrings for 24 hours in cold water, changing the water as often as possible.

2   Boil and dice the potatoes. Dice the beetroot, apple, cucumber and veal. Chop the onion. Cut the heads off the herrings; open the fish flat, pressing along the backbone; remove and discard the backbone and skin. Cut the fish into pieces.

3   Place all the ingredients in a large bowl and season with 1 tablespoon wine vinegar. Sprinkle with pepper.

4   Push the hard-boiled eggs through a fine sieve into a small bowl. Mix together 1 tablespoon wine vinegar, the mustard and a pinch of salt. Stir in the oil gradually and add the soured cream or yoghurt last.

5   Pour the mixture over the herrings, stir carefully and sprinkle with chopped dill and the sieved egg yolks. Cover and refrigerate for 3 hours. Garnish with hard-boiled eggs and lettuce.

Scallops à la provençale

Preparation: 20 minutes
 (+ 1 hour for cleaning the
 scallops)

1 kg/2¼ lb scallops
salt and pepper
50 g/2 oz butter
3 tbsp flour
2 shallots
1 tbsp oil
1 clove garlic
125 ml/4 fl oz white wine
1 tbsp chopped parsley

1 Leave the scallops under cold running water for 1 hour; prize them open and remove the white meat and coral. Reserve the shells. Discard the black gristly parts. Cut the white cushion in two and sprinkle with salt and pepper.

2 Heat 40 g/1½ oz butter in a frying pan. Lightly coat the scallops in flour and fry gently, a few at a time, for 3 minutes until golden brown. Cook the corals for 1½ to 2 minutes only.

3 Finely chop the shallots and fry for 2 minutes in the remaining butter and oil. Add the garlic, cook for one minute then add to the scallops. Pour in the wine.

4 Cook over a moderate heat for another 3 minutes.

5 Remove the scallops and keep warm. Reduce the sauce by boiling vigorously.

6 Pour the sauce over the scallops, sprinkle with chopped parsley and serve in warmed shells.

Ceviche

(Marinated fillets of sole Peruvian style)

Preparation: 40 minutes
   (+ 4 hours for marinating
   the sole)

600 g/1¼ lb sole fillets
2 lemons
½ onion
1 clove garlic
few sprigs parsley
1-2 large ripe tomatoes
1 tsp chilli powder
2 tbsp oil
salt

1   Place the fillets in a deep dish and pour over the lemon juice. Refrigerate for 4 hours, turning several times with a wooden spoon. The fish will turn white and harden.

2   Chop the onion, garlic and half of the parsley very finely.

3   Peel the tomatoes, remove the seeds, and dice.

4   Mix together in a bowl the onion, garlic, parsley, tomatoes, chilli powder and oil. Sprinkle with salt, then turn these ingredients into a serving dish.

5   Drain the fillets (reserve the lemon juice), cut into fairly large pieces and arrange decoratively on top of the seasoned tomatoes.

6   Sprinkle with a little of the reserved lemon juice and garnish with parsley.

Deep-fried oysters

Preparation: 50 minutes

24 cleaned oysters
175 ml/6 fl oz milk
salt and pepper
25 g/1 oz flour
2 eggs
125 g/4 oz breadcrumbs

1   Rinse the oysters in cold water and drain well.

2   Place the oysters in a bowl and cover with the milk; leave to stand for 15 minutes.

3   Drain the oysters thoroughly and turn on to kitchen paper; pat dry all over.

4   Season with a little salt and freshly ground pepper.

5   Roll the oysters in the flour, coating each one thoroughly.

6   Beat the eggs in a bowl with a little salt and pepper and dip each oyster into this mixture.

7   Coat the oysters in the breadcrumbs, pressing the crumbs to adhere firmly to the oyster.

8   Heat the oil in a deep frying pan or a wok; when the oil is very hot lower the oysters in carefully and fry until golden brown. Drain well and serve at once, garnished with lemon wedges, shredded lettuce and fresh parsley.

Spring rolls

Serves 6-12

125 g/4 oz lean pork or
   chicken, shredded
1¹/₂ tbsp cornflour
2 tbsp peanut oil
50 g/2 oz bamboo shoots
2 Chinese mushrooms,
   sliced
1 small leek, chopped
flour
12 Chinese pancakes*

For the sauce:
1 tbsp sugar
pinch salt
¹/₂ tbsp soy sauce
2 tsp light soy sauce
2 tbsp chicken stock
1 tbsp peanut oil
few drops sesame oil
1 tbsp flour

1   Coat the meat with the
cornflour.

2   Heat the peanut oil in a
wok and stir-fry the meat,
bamboo shoots and
mushrooms for 1 minute.
Add the sauce ingredients
and stir-fry until the liquid
evaporates; add the leek.
Transfer to a plate and cool.

3   Prepare a paste by
mixing 1 tablespoon flour
with 1 tablespoon cold water
and 2 tablespoons boiling
water.

4   Place some of the filling
along one half of each
pancake; fold the pancake
over the filling, tuck in the
edges and roll up, sealing
with the paste. Deep-fry the
rolls in hot oil (180°C/350°F).

Terrine of pork

Preparation: 1 hour

1 large onion
50 g/2 oz streaky bacon
knob of butter
2 cloves garlic
1 bay leaf
300 g/10¹/₂ oz chopped raw
    pork
pinch paprika
175 ml/6 fl oz dry white wine
175 ml/6 fl oz chicken stock
salt and pepper
1 black olive
parsley or watercress

1   Peel the onion and chop finely.

2   Cut the bacon into strips, using a very sharp knife.

3   Melt the butter and add the onion, the finely chopped garlic and the bay leaf and sauté gently.

4   Add the bacon and the chopped pork and sauté briskly over a higher heat. Add a generous pinch of paprika. Pour in the wine and cook until it has completely evaporated.

5   Add the stock and the diced breast of chicken and leave to simmer over a moderate heat until the meat is cooked through.

6   Allow the mixture to cool a little before placing in the electric blender or food processor; blend until the mixture is smooth.

7   Transfer the mixture to a bowl, season with salt and pepper and stir well.

8   Place the bowl in the refrigerator and chill for a few hours. Just before serving transfer to an earthenware dish or terrine, press down firmly and make a ribbed pattern on the surface with the prongs of a fork. Place a black olive in the centre and surround with a few flat parsley leaves or watercress.

Foie gras truffé en gelée

Preparation: 1 hour (+ 3
 hours for soaking the
 truffle)

1 large raw goose liver	*For the chicken aspic:*
1 truffle	225 g/8 oz chicken wings
2 large thin slices fresh	1 onion
pork fat	1 celery stalk
125 ml/4 fl oz brandy	1 tbsp powdered gelatine
125 ml/4 fl oz port	1.1 litres/2 pints water
1.1 litres/2 pints cold stock	
500 ml/1 pint chicken aspic	
salt and pepper	

1 Wash the truffle and scrape off the rough skin with a small sharp knife or brush. Place in a small bowl.

2 Pour the port over the truffle, followed by the brandy, and season very lightly with a pinch of salt and a little freshly ground pepper. Leave to soak for 3 hours. *To prepare the chicken aspic:* make chicken stock with the chicken trimmings, vegetables and the water, boiling gently until the liquid has reduced to 500 ml/1 pint strained volume. Dissolve the gelatine in this (do not allow to boil again).

3 Make a small, deep incision all the way to the centre of the liver and push the drained truffle into this pocket.

4 Wrap the slices of pork fat around the liver, tying with string.

5 Wrap the barded liver in cheesecloth and sew up securely with thread.

6 Place the liver in the cold stock and bring slowly to the boil; simmer gently for 20 minutes.

7 Turn off the heat and leave the liver to cool gradually in the cooking liquid; when it is cold, take up and unwrap, removing the fat.

8 Pour some of the chicken aspic into an oblong or oval dish; cover and chill in the refrigerator until just set; place the sliced goose liver on top and cover with more aspic. Return to the refrigerator to set. Chop the remaining chilled aspic and use to garnish the dish.

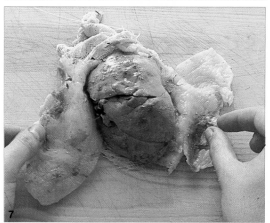

Hsao mai

(Chinese steamed dumplings)

For the filling:
350 g/³/₄ lb onions
50 g/2 oz cornflour
400 g/14 oz minced lean
  pork
20 *hsao mai* dough sheets*

Seasonings:
2 tbsp rice wine
¹/₂ tsp salt
¹/₂ tsp sugar
1 tbsp soy sauce
1 tbsp sesame oil
pinch pepper
¹/₂ tsp chopped root ginger

For the toppings:
2-3 egg yolks
peanut oil
seaweed as required
3 slices cooked ham
1 small can crab meat
3 Chinese aromatic
  mushrooms (*tung ku*
  variety), soaked in warm
  water for 30 minutes and
  chopped.

1   To prepare the scrambled eggs for the topping, heat a little peanut oil in a wok, pour in the beaten egg yolks and cook over a gentle heat, breaking up the egg yolks as they set.

2   Prepare the filling: chop the onions finely, add the cornflour and mix well.

3   Mix all the seasonings together. Place the ground pork in a bowl, add the seasoning mixture, and mix well until smooth.

4   Add the floured onion to the meat mixture; mix well.

5   Make a loose fist, thumb upward, with one hand, stretch a dumpling sheet over the hole formed by thumb and forefinger. Place some filling in the centre of the dough sheet and push down into the hole, supporting the bottom of the little bag with the little finger of the same hand.

6   When all the dough sheets are filled in this way, decorate the tops with a selection of chopped seaweed, chopped ham, scrambled egg, chopped crab meat and the dried Chinese mushrooms.

7   Brush the bottom of a bamboo steamer with a thin film of oil, arrange the *hsao mai* carefully in the steamer and place over boiling water. Cover and steam for 9 to 12 minutes.

Pasta, Rice and Cereals

Chilled spaghettini with caviar

Preparation: 20 minutes

225 g/8 oz spaghettini
salt
3 tbsp olive oil
1 tbsp chopped fresh chives
3 tbsp caviar or black
 lumpfish roe

1   Cook the spaghettini in boiling salted water for 8-10 minutes until *al dente*. Drain.

2   Leave to stand under cold running water in a colander for at least 1 minute.

3   Pour into a large bowl, add the olive oil and chopped chives and mix well.

4   Serve in individual dishes, each portion garnished with a spoonful of caviar or lumpfish roe.

Spaghettini with tomato sauce

Preparation: 30 minutes

350 g/12 oz spaghettini
¹/₂ onion
1 clove garlic
6 tbsp olive oil
400 g/14 oz ripe tomatoes
salt
black pepper
1 tbsp chopped fresh basil
fresh basil leaves

1   Finely chop the onion and garlic and fry briefly in the olive oil.

2   Skin and seed the tomatoes and chop. Sprinkle with salt and add to the onions. Cover and cook gently for 5-8 minutes.

3   Cook the spaghettini in a large saucepan of boiling salted water for 8-10 minutes until *al dente*. Drain.

4   Pour the spaghettini into the sauce; sprinkle with freshly ground black pepper, stir well and add the chopped basil.

5   Serve in heated dishes and garnish with the whole basil leaves.

Seafood spaghettini

Preparation: 50 minutes
(+ 2 hours to clean the
molluscs)

225 g/8 oz spaghettini
900 g/2 lb assorted molluscs
(mussels, clams, sea
dates)
4 uncooked Dublin Bay
prawns
salt
4 tbsp olive oil
1 ripe tomato
1 clove garlic
1 tbsp chopped fresh parsley
black pepper

1   Leave the molluscs to
stand in a colander under
cold running water for 2
hours to remove all traces of
sand. Drain and place in a
large frying pan. Cover and
heat for 3 minutes until the
shells open.

2   Remove the meat from
the shells. Reserve and
strain the cooking liquor.

3   Steam the prawns or
cook in salted water for 4
minutes.

4   Pour 3 tbsp olive oil into
a large frying pan. Skin,
seed and chop the tomato
and add to the oil. Cook for
5 minutes then add the
molluscs, prawns and
reserved liquor.

5   Pour 1 tbsp oil into a
small frying pan, add the
crushed garlic and cook over
a low heat for 2 minutes.

6   Cook the spaghettini in
boiling salted water for 8-10
minutes until *al dente*. Drain
and pour into the frying pan
with the tomato sauce and
molluscs. Sprinkle with
freshly ground black pepper,
chopped parsley and the
garlic-flavoured oil. Mix well
before serving.

Spaghetti alla carbonara

Preparation: 30 minutes

275 g/10 oz spaghetti
125 g/4 oz pancetta or
   bacon
1 tbsp olive oil
1 clove garlic
2 eggs
salt
black pepper
2 tbsp grated Parmesan
2 tbsp grated Pecorino
   cheese or mature
   Cheddar

1   Cut the bacon into small dice.

2   Heat the olive oil in a small saucepan, add the crushed garlic and bacon and brown gently for 3 minutes. Discard the garlic.

3   Cook the spaghetti in boiling salted water for 10-12 minutes until *al dente*. Drain.

4   Beat together the eggs, salt, freshly ground black pepper and grated cheeses and pour into a very hot soup tureen.

5   Pour the spaghetti into the tureen.

6   Add the browned bacon and any remaining oil. Stir well before serving.

Spaghettini with garlic, oil and chilli pepper

Preparation: 20 minutes

350 g/12 oz spaghettini
4 cloves garlic
175 ml/6 fl oz olive oil
$^1/_2$ red chilli pepper
salt
1 tbsp chopped fresh parsley

1 Skin and finely dice the cloves of garlic. Place in a large frying pan with the olive oil.

2 Cut the chilli pepper into very fine rings, discarding the seeds, and add to the pan with the garlic. Fry *very* gently for 2 minutes.

3 Cook the spaghettini in boiling salted water for 8-10 minutes until *al dente*.

4 Drain and pour into the frying pan. Add the chopped parsley and mix well for 2 minutes over heat before serving.

Bucatini all'amatriciana

Preparation: 30 minutes

350 g/12 oz bucatini
125 g/4 oz bacon
275 g/10 oz ripe tomatoes
2 tbsp olive oil
salt
$^{1}/_{2}$ clove garlic
2 leaves fresh basil
$^{1}/_{2}$ red chilli pepper
3 tbsp grated Parmesan
3 tbsp grated mature
   Pecorino or mature
   Cheddar.

1   Cut the rind off the bacon and cut into 5 × 40-mm/$^{1}/_{4}$ × 1$^{1}/_{2}$-in strips.

2   Prepare the tomato sauce: skin, seed and coarsely chop the tomatoes. Heat in a frying pan for 10 minutes with the olive oil, a little salt and the garlic. Add the basil and cook for a further 5 minutes.

3   Remove the garlic and basil and sieve the tomatoes.

4   Gently brown the bacon in no extra oil with the finely chopped chilli pepper.

5   Cook the bucatini in plenty of boiling salted water for 10-12 minutes until *al dente*. Drain.

6   Pour the bucatini into a heated serving dish. Sprinkle with the bacon and any fat in the frying pan, the tomato sauce and grated cheeses. Stir, cover and leave to stand for 3 minutes before serving.

Bucatini with broccoli

Preparation: 30 minutes

275 g/10 oz bucatini
800 g/1³/₄ lb broccoli
salt
6 tbsp olive oil
¹/₄ red chilli pepper
1 clove garlic
50 g/2 oz salted anchovies

1   Rinse and trim the broccoli, keeping only the tops.

2   Cook them in boiling salted water for 8-10 minutes until tender but still crisp. Drain, reserving the water, and keep warm.

3   Cook the bucatini in the reserved water for 10-12 minutes.

4   When almost *al dente* return the broccoli to the water. Drain after 2 minutes.

5   Pour the olive oil into a large frying pan. Add the chopped chilli pepper, the finely diced garlic and the rinsed, boned and chopped anchovies.

6   Heat for 3 minutes then add the bucatini and broccoli. Stir gently for 1 minute then serve. Sprinkle with grated Parmesan if desired.

Fettuccine with ham and cream cheese

Preparation: 20 minutes

350 g/12 oz fettuccine
salt
50 g/2 oz cooked ham, in
  one slice
125 g/4 oz mascarpone
  (cream cheese)
2-3 tbsp grated Parmesan
black pepper

1   Cook the fettuccine in boiling salted water for 6 minutes until *al dente*. Drain.

2   Cut the ham into thin strips. Heat for a few minutes in a saucepan with 1 tbsp cream cheese.

3   Mix together the remaining cream cheese, Parmesan and a little freshly ground black pepper in a warm serving dish and stir well.

4   Add the piping hot fettuccine and the strips of ham. Stir well and serve.

Penne with peppers and courgettes

Preparation: 30 minutes

275 g/10 fl oz fluted penne
1 sweet yellow pepper
2 small courgettes
25 g/1 oz butter
salt
225 ml/8 fl oz freshly made
　tomato sauce*
4 courgette flowers
25 g/1 oz flour
150 ml/5 fl oz vegetable oil
1 tbsp chopped fresh parsley
black pepper

1　Scorch the pepper over a high heat until the skin blisters, then rub the skin off.

2　Peel the courgettes and cut them and the pepper into small dice.

3　Melt the butter in a large frying pan; add the diced pepper and fry for 5 minutes. Add the courgettes, sprinkle with salt and fry until the vegetables are tender but still crisp. Stir in the tomato sauce.

4　Dip the courgette flowers in flour and fry briefly in vegetable oil. Drain. Sprinkle with salt.

5　Cook the penne in plenty of boiling salted water for 10-12 minutes until *al dente*.

6　Drain and add to the pan with the vegetables. Stir and sprinkle with chopped parsley and freshly ground black pepper. Garnish each serving with a fried courgette flower.

Penne with black olives and tomatoes

Preparation: 30 minutes

275 g/10 oz penne
350 g/12 oz ripe tomatoes
4 tbsp olive oil
salt
125 g/4 oz black olives
¹/₂ tsp oregano
1 tbsp grated Pecorino or
   Parmesan cheese
black pepper
4 leaves fresh basil

1   Skin the tomatoes and discard the seeds.

2   Chop coarsely and heat in the olive oil in a large frying pan. Sprinkle with salt.

3   After 6 minutes, add the stoned olives and the oregano. Cook for a further 5 minutes.

4   Cook the penne in boiling salted water for 10-12 minutes until *al dente*. Drain.

5   Add the penne to the tomatoes and olives. Sprinkle with the cheese and freshly ground black pepper and stir well over high heat for 2 minutes.

6   Turn into a heated serving dish and garnish with fresh basil.

Penne with clams and peas

Preparation: 40 minutes
(+2 hours to clean the clams)

275 g/10 oz fluted penne
400 g/14 oz clams
400 g/14 oz peas
4 tbsp olive oil
salt
1 tbsp chopped fresh parsley
black pepper

1   Leave the clams in a colander under cold running water for 2 hours to remove all traces of sand.

2   Drain and heat for 2-3 minutes in a large covered frying pan over a high heat until the shells open.

3   Remove the clams from their shells. Strain and reserve the cooking liquor.

4   Shell the peas and simmer for 12 minutes in a large pan with the olive oil and 6 tbsp of the reserved liquor. Season with salt.

5   Cook the penne in boiling salted water for 10-12 minutes until *al dente.* Drain.

6   Add the clams to the peas and cook for a further 2 minutes. Add salt if necessary. Pour in the penne, sprinkle with chopped parsley and black pepper and mix well for 1 minute before serving.

45

Maltagliati with duck

Preparation: 2 hours

1 duckling, cleaned, liver
　reserved
3 carrots
1 onion
1 celery stalk
1 tbsp chopped fresh parsley
275 ml/10 fl oz red wine
salt
pepper
125 g/4 oz courgettes
1 tbsp olive oil
50 g/2 oz butter
16 black olives, stoned
350 g/12 oz maltagliati

For the pasta:
225 g/8 oz flour
2 eggs
1 egg yolk
salt

Maltagliati are thin sheets of
pasta cut into triangles. They
are used in various soups
and main-course dishes.

1   Prepare the pasta dough* by mixing together the flour, eggs, salt and a little water. Roll out in a thin sheet and cut into rectangles, then triangles, using a sharp knife.

2   Using a sharp knife, carefully cut away the breast fillets from the duck.

3   Roughly chop the rest of the carcass into pieces and place in a saucepan with one carrot, the onion, celery and chopped parsley. Add the red wine and simmer for about 15 minutes until slightly reduced.

4   Strain the stock and adjust the seasoning. Add the crushed reserved duck liver and cook for a few more minutes.

5   Cut the courgettes and remaining carrots into thin strips and blanch in boiling salted water for a couple of minutes.

6   Brown the duck breast fillets briefly in the olive oil; sprinkle with salt and pepper and cook for a few minutes so that the meat is still pink.

7   Leave to cool slightly then cut into small pieces.

8   Cook the maltagliati in boiling salted water for 2-3 minutes only, then drain. Put the sauce, butter, vegetables, sliced duck, halved olives and drained maltagliati into a large frying pan. Season with salt and pepper and stir well for a few minutes over a moderate heat before serving.

Country-style macaroni

Preparation: 20 minutes

275 g/10 oz macaroni
salt
3 egg yolks
4 tbsp grated Parmesan
125 g/4 oz mascarpone
  (cream cheese)
black pepper
nutmeg

1   Cook the macaroni in
boiling salted water for
10-12 minutes until *al dente*.
Drain.

2   Mix the egg yolks with
the grated Parmesan in a
large, very hot tureen.

3   Place the tureen over a
saucepan of boiling water so
that it is heated by the
steam.

4   Add the mascarpone, a
generous sprinkling of
freshly ground black pepper
and a pinch of nutmeg. Stir
well.

5   Pour in the very hot
macaroni and mix well over
heat before serving.

Macaroni with four cheeses

Preparation: 30 minutes

275 g/10 oz macaroni
salt
50 g/2 oz Gorgonzola
50 g/2 oz Fontina or Edam
50 g/2 oz Emmenthal
25 g/1 oz butter
4 tbsp grated Parmesan
black pepper

1   Cook the macaroni in boiling salted water for 10-12 minutes until *al dente*.

2   Drain well and transfer to a buttered flameproof dish.

3   Dice the cheeses and sprinkle evenly over the top.

4   Place in a preheated oven, at 170°C/325°F/mark 3, for 6 minutes.

5   Remove from the oven, add the butter and sprinkle with the grated Parmesan and plenty of freshly ground black pepper. Stir well for 2 minutes over a high heat before serving.

Macaroni with fresh sardines and dill

Preparation: 1 hour (+ 30 minutes for soaking the sultanas)

2-3 tbsp sultanas
125 g/4 oz fresh dill
salt and pepper
350 g/12 oz fresh sardines
1 large onion
4 tbsp oil
3 tomatoes
50 g/2 oz pine nuts
4 anchovy fillets
225 g/8 oz macaroni

1   Soak the sultanas in warm water for 30 minutes. Trim and wash the dill weed, reserving the feathery green leaves. Cook the dill in plenty of salted water for 10 minutes. Drain well, reserving the water, and chop.

2   Clean and rinse the sardines; cut off the heads, open out flat, and pat dry with kitchen paper.

3   Fry the finely chopped onion in the oil for 5 minutes in a large frying pan. Add the seeded and chopped tomatoes, pine nuts, and drained sultanas.

4   Cook for a further 5 minutes, then add the sardines and chopped dill. Season with salt and pepper, cover and simmer for 10 minutes.

5   Add the finely chopped anchovy fillets and cook for another 5 minutes.

6   Bring the reserved cooking water to the boil and cook the macaroni for 10 to 12 minutes or until *al dente.* Drain well and mix gently with the sardine, anchovy and tomato mixture.

Pasta spirals with mussels and potatoes

Preparation: 40 minutes
  (+ 2 hours to clean the
  mussels)

225 g/8 oz pasta spirals
500 g/1 lb mussels
225 g/8 oz potatoes
salt
125 ml/4 fl oz olive oil
pepper
1 tbsp chopped fresh parsley

1 Leave the mussels for 2 hours under cold running water.

2 Drain well and place in a large covered frying pan over a high heat for 3 minutes until the shells open.

3 Remove the mussels from their shells. Discard any that do not open. Strain and reserve the liquor.

4 Peel and slice the potatoes and cut into pieces.

5 Boil in salted water for 5-8 minutes or until tender. Drain.

6 Heat the olive oil in a large pan. Add the mussels and potatoes and cook for 2 minutes. Add 6 tbsp of the reserved liquor.

7 Cook the pasta spirals in boiling salted water for 10-12 minutes until *al dente*.

8 Drain and pour into the pan; sprinkle with pepper and chopped parsley and stir before serving.

Trenette with pesto (basil sauce)

Preparation: 1 hour

275 g/10 oz trenette (or
  spaghetti)
125 g/4 oz potatoes
50 g/2 oz green beans
salt
6 tbsp pesto sauce*
2 tbsp grated Pecorino or
  Parmesan

1   Peel, rinse and cut the
potatoes into cubes. Rinse
and slice the beans.

2   Cook the vegetables in
boiling salted water until
tender. Drain, reserving the
cooking water, and keep
hot.

3   Cook the trenette in the
reserved water for 8-10
minutes or until *al dente*.

4   Drain and add to the
vegetables. Stir in the pesto
and grated cheese and mix
well before serving.

Baked spinach lasagna

Preparation: 1 hour 20
    minutes

275 g/10 oz spinach lasagna

For the meat sauce:
25 g/1 oz bacon
1 tbsp chopped onion
$^1/_2$ carrot
$^1/_2$ celery stalk
80 g/3 oz butter
125 g/4 oz pork sausage
125 g/4 oz beef
50 g/2 oz ham
1 tbsp freshly made tomato
    sauce*
50 g/2 oz chicken livers
2-3 tbsp single cream
black pepper
225 g/8 oz grated Parmesan

For the white sauce:
50 g/2 oz butter
40 g/1$^1/_2$ oz flour
500 ml/18 fl oz milk
white pepper

For the pasta:
225 g/8 oz flour
2 eggs and 1 egg yolk
125 g/4 oz cooked spinach

1   Chop the bacon, onion, carrot and celery.

2   Brown gently in 50 g/2 oz butter, then add the ground pork sausage, beef and ham.

3   Cook for another 3 minutes, then add the tomato sauce diluted in a ladleful of hot water. Add salt and simmer gently for 40 minutes, adding more water if necessary.

4   Prepare the spinach lasagna*, combining the flour, eggs, a pinch of salt and the cooked and puréed spinach. Roll out and cut into wide strips, then into squares.

5   Cook the lasagna sheets for 3-5 minutes in plenty of boiling salted water (add 1 tbsp olive oil to prevent them from sticking together). When they are *al dente*, drain and rinse with cold water to prevent further cooking. Place in a single layer on a clean teacloth to dry.

6   Prepare the white sauce: melt the butter, add the flour and stir for 3 minutes. Stir in the hot milk gradually and cook for about 10 minutes. Season with salt and pepper.

7   Cut the chicken livers into small pieces and add to the meat sauce. Cook for 3 minutes, then stir in the cream. Simmer for 4 minutes, adjust the seasoning and sprinkle with a little freshly ground black pepper.

8   Butter an ovenproof dish and place a layer of lasagna in the bottom. Sprinkle with a little grated Parmesan, then with meat sauce, followed by white sauce. Repeat the procedure, making a second layer, then finish with a layer of lasagna. Cover with a thin layer of white sauce, sprinkle with Parmesan and a few flakes of butter. Bake in a preheated oven at 180°C/350°F/mark 4 for about 20 minutes.

Ham and cheese cannelloni

Preparation: 1 hour 10
   minutes

600 g-800 g/1¹/₄-1³/₄ lb
   cannelloni
salt
1 tbsp olive oil
50 g/2 oz butter
40 g/1¹/₂ oz flour
280 ml/¹/₂ pint milk
white pepper

For the pasta:
275 g/10 oz flour
3 eggs

For the filling:
225 g/8 oz ricotta
3 tbsp grated Parmesan
125 g/4 oz cooked ham
salt, black pepper

1   Prepare a sheet of pasta
by combining the flour and
eggs. Roll the dough out
very thinly and cut into
10-cm/4-in squares.

2   Cook in boiling salted
water for 3-5 minutes with 1
tbsp olive oil to prevent
them sticking. Drain
carefully when *al dente* and
spread out on a clean cloth.

3   Mix together in a bowl
the ricotta, Parmesan, diced
ham, salt and pepper.

4   Place some of the filling
on each square and roll up
into cannelloni.

5   Melt the butter and stir in
the flour. Gradually add the
hot milk, then simmer for 10
minutes, stirring
occasionally. Season with
salt and white pepper.

6   Place the cannelloni in a
buttered ovenproof dish.
Pour over the white sauce
and place in a preheated
oven, at 170°C/325°F/mark
3, for 8 minutes before
serving.

Tagliatelle au gratin

Preparation: 1 hour 10
   minutes

400 g/14 oz green tagliatelle
80 g/3 oz butter
40 g/1¹/₂ oz flour
350 ml/12 fl oz milk
salt
white pepper
4 tbsp grated Parmesan

For the pasta:
275 g/10 oz flour
500 g/1 lb spinach
3 eggs
salt

1   Melt 40 g/1¹/₂ oz butter in
a saucepan. Stir in the flour
and gradually add the hot
milk; cook for 10 minutes,
stirring constantly. Season
with salt and white pepper.

2   Cook the tagliatelle* in
boiling salted water for 3
minutes until *al dente.*

3   Butter an ovenproof dish
and pour in one third of the
tagliatelle. Cover with one
third of the white sauce and
Parmesan. Continue
layering until all the
ingredients are used up.

4   Dot the remaining butter
on top and bake in a
preheated oven at
170°C/350°F/mark 3 for 8
minutes before serving.

Tagliatelle with sole and saffron

Preparation: 1 hour 10
  minutes

275 g/10 oz fresh tagliatelle
275 g/10 oz sole fillet
50 g/2 oz butter
4 fresh chives
salt
2 tbsp white wine
4 tbsp fumet*
pinch saffron threads
black pepper

For the pasta:
200 g/7 oz flour
2 eggs
salt

1   Rinse and dry the sole
and cut into thin strips.

2   Melt half the butter in a
large frying pan. Add the
chives and sole; sprinkle
with salt, pour over the
white wine, then cover and
simmer for 4 minutes.

3   Heat the fumet and add
the saffron threads.

4   Pour the fumet into the
frying pan and simmer for a
further 2 minutes. Discard
the chives, add the
remaining butter and
simmer for a further 2
minutes.

5   Cook the tagliatelle* in
boiling salted water for 3
minutes until *al dente*.
Drain.

6   Pour the tagliatelle into
the pan. Sprinkle with
pepper and mix carefully
before serving.

Pappardelle with partridge

Preparation: 1 hour 40
   minutes (+ 6 hours for
   the pasta to dry)

2 partridges
2 rashers streaky bacon
2 sprigs rosemary
40 g/1½ oz butter
1 tbsp olive oil
salt
black pepper
4 juniper berries
25 g/1 oz chopped onion
½ celery stalk
150 ml/5 fl oz white wine
50 g/2 oz truffle

350 g/12 oz pappardelle

For the pasta:
225 g/8 oz flour
2 eggs and 1 egg yolk
salt

Pappardelle are wide strips
of pasta traditionally served
with meat sauces.

1   Prepare the pasta dough* by mixing together the flour, eggs and a pinch of salt. Roll into a thin sheet, cut into 2-cm/³/₄-in-wide strips and leave to dry for at least 6 hours.

2   Clean, singe and rinse the partridges. Pat dry with kitchen paper.

3   Wrap a rasher of bacon round each sprig of rosemary and place one inside each partridge.

4   Heat the butter and olive oil in a large saucepan and brown the partridges on all sides. Season with salt and freshly ground black pepper.

5   Add the juniper berries, the chopped onion and celery and pour over the wine. As the wine evaporates add a few tablespoons of hot water or stock.

6   When the partridges are cooked, remove all the meat and shred. Keep the meat hot.

7   Break the carcasses with a cleaver and place in a saucepan with cooking juices. Add 4 tablespoons hot water and cook for 10 minutes. Strain through a fine sieve, reserving the stock.

8   Cook the pappardelle in boiling salted water for 4 minutes until *al dente*. Drain, then transfer to a saucepan with the reserved stock and meat. Stir well. Serve in individual dishes and sprinkle with slivers of truffle, thinly sliced with a mandoline cutter.

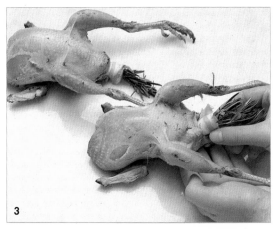

Tagliolini with chicken livers

Preparation: 30 minutes

275 g/10 oz egg tagliolini*
125 g/4 oz chicken livers
225 g/8 oz tinned tomatoes
1 sprig rosemary
salt
pinch sugar
1 tbsp olive oil
40 g/1¹/₂ oz butter
2 fresh sage leaves
pepper

1   Trim the fat from the livers.

2   Cut into 1-cm/¹/₂-in pieces. Rinse under running water for 1 minute then dry well.

3   Purée the tomatoes in a blender and cook in a small saucepan for 7 minutes with the rosemary, salt, sugar and 1 tbsp olive oil.

4   Melt the butter in a large saucepan. Stir in the sage and chicken livers and cook for 2-3 minutes over a low heat.

5   Cook the tagliolini in boiling salted water for 6 minutes or until *al dente*. Drain well.

6   Remove the rosemary from the hot tomato sauce. Pour the sauce over the chicken livers.

7   Place the saucepan over a moderate heat, add the tagliolini, season with pepper and stir well before serving.

Tagliolini with mushrooms

Preparation: 1 hour

350 g/12 oz tagliolini*
350 g/12 oz *porcini*
    mushrooms
salt
125 ml/4 fl oz olive oil
1 clove garlic
6 leaves fresh basil
1 tbsp chopped fresh parsley
1 tbsp grated Parmesan
black pepper

For the pasta:
275 g/10 oz flour
3 eggs
salt

1   Wash the mushrooms in salted water; drain and then slice.

2   Heat 4 tbsp olive oil in a large pan and gently fry the mushrooms for 5-8 minutes or until tender. Sprinkle with salt.

3   Cook the tagliolini* in plenty of boiling salted water for 3-4 minutes if freshly made, for 6 minutes if dried. Drain.

4   Brown the finely diced garlic in the remaining oil over a low heat for 2 minutes.

5   Pour the tagliolini into the pan containing the mushrooms, keeping the heat low. Add the garlic and oil, the finely chopped basil and parsley and the grated Parmesan. Stir well, adding a little of the cooking water from the tagliolini if necessary. Sprinkle with freshly ground black pepper before serving.

Paella valenciana

Preparation: 1 hour 40
    minutes

$^1/_2$ onion
1 green or yellow pepper
2 tomatoes
$^1/_2$ small chicken
125 g/4 oz pork tenderloin
125 ml/4 fl oz oil
1 clove garlic
125 g/4 oz spicy sausage
salt and pepper
1 packet saffron powder
1 bay leaf
500 ml/8 fl oz stock or water
4 uncooked Dublin Bay
    prawns
16 mussels

125 g/4 oz pilaf rice
125 g/4 oz shelled peas
pinch chilli powder

1   Chop the onion. Char the pepper under the grill; plunge into cold water and rub off the skin. Discard the seeds and cut the pepper into thin strips. Peel the tomatoes, remove the seeds, and chop. Cut the chicken into pieces and dice the pork.

2   Heat 2 tablespoons oil in a frying pan and brown the chicken and pork for 10 minutes. Remove and set aside. Put the sausage in the same pan, prick with a fork and fry for 10 minutes. Set aside with the meat.

3   Add 1 tablespoon oil to the pan and fry the onion and crushed garlic briefly. Remove the garlic as soon as it begins to brown. When the onion begins to brown add the tomatoes. Add salt to taste and cook for 10 minutes.

4   Place the scrubbed mussels in a saucepan, cover, and cook over a high heat for 5 minutes until the shells open.

5   Place the chicken, pork, sausage and bay leaf in another saucepan with 500 ml/8 fl oz stock and simmer for 15 minutes.

6   Cook the Dublin Bay prawns in boiling salted water for 3 minutes. Drain.

7   Heat 3 tablespoons oil in a large paella pan or cast-iron pan and brown the rice, stirring with a wooden spoon. Gradually stir in the cooking liquid from the meat, the strips of pepper, and the shelled peas and cook for about 15 minutes or until the rice is tender. Dissolve the saffron in a little warm water and stir into the rice.

8   Stir in all the remaining ingredients. Mix well and place in a hot oven for 5 minutes before serving.

Fisherman's risotto

Preparation: 45 minutes

400 g/14 oz risotto rice
   (arborio)
225 g/8 oz squid
1 small onion
175 ml/6 fl oz oil
2-3 tbsp finely chopped
   parsley
1.1 litres/2 pints fish stock*
2 tbsp tomato purée
1 green pepper
1 clove garlic
1 packet saffron
50 g/2 oz cooked peas
225 g/8 oz eel
12 clams
225 g/8 oz monkfish
8 peeled prawns
salt and pepper

1   Wash and trim the assorted fish; cut the squid into rings.

2   Sauté the squid in the oil in a heavy-bottomed saucepan.

3   Add the finely chopped onion and sauté gently until it begins to colour.

4   Mix the tomato purée with 125 ml/4 fl oz hot water and add to the saucepan; add the eel (skinned and cut into pieces), the monkfish and prawns.

5   Simmer for a few minutes and then add the rice.

6   Stir gently, adding the hot fish stock a little at a time, then add the seeded, trimmed and diced green pepper, the peas, clams, saffron (dissolved in a little stock), and finely chopped garlic. Add a little salt and freshly ground pepper to taste. Simmer until the rice is tender but still firm, stirring frequently. Sprinkle with the chopped parsley and serve immediately.

Risotto with quails

Preparation: 1 hour 15
   minutes

8 quails	*For the risotto:*
8 thin slices streaky bacon or fresh pork fat	500 g/1 lb risotto rice (arborio)
50 g/2 oz butter	40 g/1½ oz butter
1 small celery stalk	2 tbsp oil
few spoonfuls light stock	850 ml/1½ pints light stock
175 ml/6 fl oz brandy	1 finely chopped onion
1 spring onion	4 tbsp freshly grated Parmesan cheese
1 carrot	175 ml/6 fl oz dry white wine
salt and pepper	salt
optional: 1 small white truffle to grate	

1   Wash and dry the quails; season inside each with a pinch of salt, freshly ground pepper and a little grated truffle and sprinkle with the brandy, if desired.

2   Truss each bird and wrap in a piece of fat, securing with cocktail sticks.

3   Heat the butter in a large, heavy-bottomed saucepan and fry the quails together with the finely chopped spring onions, celery, and carrot.

4   Cook the quails over a gentle heat for about 50 minutes, adding a few spoonfuls of stock to moisten every now and then.

5   To prepare the risotto:while the quails are cooking, heat 25 g/1 oz of the butter and the oil in a deep pan and sauté the finely chopped onion gently until it is a very pale golden brown.

6   Add the rice and stir well so that the grains absorb the flavours of the butter, oil and onion. Pour in the white wine and stir until it has been absorbed or has evaporated.

7   Add about 225 ml/8 fl oz of boiling stock and continue cooking, adding more hot stock whenever it is needed. Make sure the rice does not stick to the bottom of the pan. Add a little salt if necessary.

8   When the rice is tender but still firm and the risotto is very moist, turn off the heat and stir in the grated Parmesan cheese and the remaining butter. Transfer to a heated serving platter; remove the fat from the birds and place on top of the risotto. Pour the remaining cooking liquid over the quails and serve piping hot.

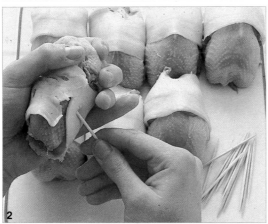

Rice with "caponata"

Preparation: 1 hour 30 minutes

4 aubergines
salt
2 medium onions
2 yellow peppers
4 courgettes
6 tomatoes
250 ml/8 fl oz olive oil
pepper
few leaves basil

175 g/6 oz black and green olives
8 anchovy fillets in oil, chopped
350 g/12 oz long-grain rice, cooked
¹/₂ lemon
1 clove garlic, crushed
1 bunch parsley

1   Wash and trim the aubergines; dice, place on a clean tea towel and sprinkle with salt. Leave to stand for 30 minutes. Peel and slice the onions, chop the peppers and slice the courgettes. Skin and chop the tomatoes.

2   Fry the onions until soft in half the oil in a pan. Add the aubergines and peppers. After 10 minutes add the courgettes and the tomatoes, skinned and diced. Season and simmer for 35-40 minutes. When cooked, add the basil, stoned olives and anchovies.

Leave the "caponata" to cool.

3   Dress the rice with oil, salt and pepper and the juice of ¹/₂ lemon. Add the garlic, chopped parsley, capers and a few basil leaves. Arrange on a serving dish with the caponata in the middle.

Rice Spanish style

Preparation: 1 hour 30
  minutes

1 small chicken or poussin
  weighing 500-700 g/
  1-1¹/₂ lb
80 g/3 oz butter
125 ml/4 fl oz olive oil
50 ml/2 fl oz brandy
salt and pepper
1³/₄ litres/3 pints stock
¹/₄ Savoy cabbage
2 carrots
1 leek
1 onion
250 g/8 oz long-grain rice
3 egg yolks
2 tbsp soy sauce
2 tbsp chopped parsley

1   Brown the chicken
evenly in a saucepan in
25 g/1 oz butter and 3 tbsp
oil. Sprinkle with brandy
and leave to evaporate. Add
salt and pepper; cover and
cook for 40 minutes, adding
stock as necessary.

2   Cut the vegetables into
thin strips. Fry the onions in
25 g/1 oz butter + 2 tbsp oil
in a large saucepan. Add the
vegetables and fry gently
over a low heat for 10
minutes, stirring
occasionally. Season with
salt and pepper; add 250 ml/
8 fl oz stock and cook for
about 25 minutes.

3   Bone the chicken and
cut the meat into even
pieces. Cook the rice in the
stock until tender, then
drain. Add the meat and rice
to the vegetables, and stir.

4   Mix the egg yolks and
soy sauce in a small bowl
and pour over the other
ingredients. Add the parsley
and stir briefly over a low
heat until creamy.

71

Prawn risotto

Preparation: 1 hour

400 g/14 oz prawns
1 carrot
1 celery stalk
salt and pepper
$^1/_2$ onion
50 g/2 oz butter
2 tbsp oil
500 g/1 lb risotto rice
    (arborio)
125 ml/4 fl oz white wine
4 tbsp chopped parsley

1   Peel the prawns.

2   Boil the heads and tails for 5 minutes in 5 ladles of water with the sliced carrot, celery and a pinch of salt.

3   Crush the heads with a wooden spoon and pour the stock through a sieve.

4   Finely chop the onion. Melt half the butter in a saucepan and cook the onion, adding 125 ml/4 fl oz water and a pinch of salt.

5   Melt the remaining butter in a pan, add the oil and prawns; sprinkle with salt and cook gently for 5 minutes.

6   When the onion is transparent, not brown, add the rice and the wine and stir over a high heat for 2 minutes.

7   Once the rice is evenly coated, add the stock and cook over a moderate heat, without stirring, until the rice is almost tender. Just before turning off the heat, add the prawns and sprinkle with pepper. The risotto should be very moist.

8   Turn off the heat, add a little extra butter and the chopped parsley and mix well with a wooden spoon. Cover and leave to stand for at least 2 minutes before serving.

Rice sartù

Preparation: 2 hours

225 g/8 oz minced beef
3 eggs
6 tbsp grated Parmesan
breadcrumbs
salt and pepper
flour
oil for frying
1 onion
25 g/1 oz mushrooms
125 g/4 oz sausage
125 g/4 oz frozen peas
2 tbsp tomato purée
1.5 litres/2$^{1}/_{2}$ pints stock
500 g/1 lb long-grain rice
25 g/1 oz butter
175 g/6 oz chicken livers
1 mozzarella cheese

1   Mix together the minced beef, 1 egg, 3 tbsp grated Parmesan, 1 tbsp breadcrumbs. Season and shape into walnut-sized balls; dip in flour and fry for a few minutes in very hot oil. Chop the onion and fry in 2 tbsp oil. Add the mushrooms, the crumbled sausage and the peas. Stir in 2 tbsp tomato purée mixed with 2 ladles stock; season and simmer for 20 minutes.

2   Pour half the sauce into a saucepan; add the rice, then cook for 15 minutes, gradually adding the remaining stock (about 1$^{1}/_{4}$ litres/2$^{1}/_{4}$ pints).

3   Turn off the heat and add the remaining Parmesan and 2 eggs. Stir.

4   Butter a high-sided mould and sprinkle with breadcrumbs.

5   Pour in three quarters of the rice then press rice around the edges using a wooden spoon.

6   Fry the chicken livers for a few minutes in 25 g/1 oz butter. Add the meatballs to the remaining rice and fill the centre of the mould with layers of sauce and meatballs, sliced mozzarella and fried chicken livers. Sprinkle each layer with a little grated cheese. Cover with the remaining rice. Cook at 170°C/325°F/mark 3 for 30 minutes. Unmould to serve.

Rice with anchovies

Preparation: 1 hour (+ 30 minutes for soaking the sultanas)

125 g/4 oz basmati rice
salt
1 large onion
50 g/2 oz butter
1 tbsp sultanas
ground allspice
$^1/_2$ tsp powdered cinnamon
$^1/_2$ tsp sugar
800 g/1$^3/_4$ lb fresh anchovies
1 tbsp pine nuts

1   Soak the rice for 30 minutes in warm salted water. Soak the sultanas in a little water.

2   Finely slice the onion and brown gently in half the butter.

3   Drain the rice and add to the onion. Fry for 5 minutes, stirring constantly.

4   Add a ladle of hot water, the drained sultanas, plenty of ground allspice, the cinnamon, sugar and salt. Cook for another 5 minutes.

5   Clean the anchovies, remove the heads and bones, and sprinkle with salt.

6   Butter a large ovenproof dish and cover with a layer of anchovies. Cover with the rice and the remaining anchovies; sprinkle with pine nuts, dot with the remaining butter and place in a preheated oven at 180°C/350°F/mark 4 for 10 minutes.

Fish soup with rice

Preparation: 1 hour
20 minutes

1 carrot
1 small onion
1 kg/2¹/₄ lb fish trimmings,
    preferably sole (heads,
    tails, bones)
1 bouquet garni
salt and pepper
50 g/2 oz rice
2 eggs
juice of ¹/₂ large lemon
1 vegetable stock cube

1   Chop the carrot and
onion and place in a
saucepan with the fish
trimmings and bouquet
garni. Add 1 litre/1³/₄ pints
water and salt to taste.
Cover and simmer gently for
10 minutes, stirring
occasionally.

2   Add another 1 litre/1³/₄
pints water and simmer for a
further 20 minutes.

3   Strain the fish stock,
pressing to obtain as much
liquid as possible, and boil
rapidly for 15 minutes to
reduce.

4   Add the rice and cook
for 15 minutes or until
tender.

5   Beat together the eggs,
lemon juice, and a ladle of
stock in a bowl. Add salt and
pepper.

6   Pour egg mixture into
the soup and simmer gently
for 3 minutes, stirring
constantly. Do not allow to
boil.

7   Remove from the heat,
cover, and leave to stand for
1 minute before serving.

Pilaf with lamb Turkish style

Serves 6

Preparation: 2 hours (+ 2½ hours for soaking the rice)

1.1 kg/2½ lb leg of lamb, cut into cubes
pinch cinnamon
175 g/6 oz butter
500 g/1 lb rice
1.1 litres/2 pints boiling stock made with stock cubes
1 finely chopped onion
50 g/2 oz pine nuts
25 g/1 oz sultanas (soaked)

6 large ripe skinned tomatoes (tinned tomatoes may be used)
225 g/8 oz lamb's liver
1 tbsp finely chopped parsley
pinch sugar
salt and pepper

1   Wash the rice in a sieve under cold water, transfer to a bowl and cover with hot water; leave to stand for $2^{1}/_{2}$ hours.

2   Sauté the lamb in a pan for 15 minutes in 125 g/4 oz butter, until the pieces have browned evenly. Season with salt and transfer to an ovenproof casserole; place in a preheated oven 180°C/350°F/mark 4 for $1^{1}/_{2}$ hours, moistening occasionally with a few spoonfuls of hot stock.

3   Sauté the chopped onion in 50 g/2 oz butter in a saucepan. Add the drained sultanas and the pine nuts and continue cooking for a few minutes.

4   Crush the tomatoes with a fork. Add to the saucepan; pour in all the stock except for 225 ml/8 fl oz and season with salt, pepper, a pinch of sugar and cinnamon.

5   Simmer for a few minutes and then add the soaked drained rice, cover tightly and place in the oven, still at 180°C/350°F/mark 4 and cook until the rice is tender.

6   While the rice is cooking, sauté the trimmed, washed and chopped liver in 3 tablespoons butter, add a pinch of salt and when the rice is ready, mix in the liver and parsley. Spoon the rice pilaf into the centre of a heated serving platter, arrange the cooked lamb around it and serve at once.

Jambalaya

Preparation: 50 minutes

275 g/10 oz long-grain rice
350 g/12 oz prawns
225 g/8 oz diced ham
4 tbsp oil
50 g/2 oz butter
1 clove garlic
1/2 onion
1 celery stalk
4 large ripe tomatoes

1 green pepper
1 bay leaf
1 clove
2 tbsp tomato purée
600 ml/1 pint stock
225 ml/8 fl oz dry white wine
oregano
salt and pepper

Jambalaya is typical of Cajun cooking in Louisiana. Rice is grown in great quantities in that area and the local seafood is highly prized. The other ingredients may vary, according to what is in season.

1   The prawns should be raw and very fresh. Peel them and chop coarsely. (If only cooked prawns are available, peel and heat only briefly).

2   Heat the oil in a pan and cook the chopped shellfish and diced ham over a high heat for a few minutes. Remove from the heat.

3   Chop the onion finely and sauté in 40 g/1½ oz butter until tender and transparent.

4   Add the washed and drained rice and cook over a low heat for a few minutes, stirring and turning so that it absorbs the flavour of the butter and onion.

5   Stir in the shellfish and ham, together with the finely chopped celery and green pepper, the finely crumbled bay leaf, the clove, the peeled and crushed garlic, a pinch of oregano, and the peeled, seeded and coarsely chopped tomatoes.

6   Season with salt and freshly ground pepper and stir for a few minutes. Bring the stock to the boil separately; stir in the tomato purée and pour over the rice. Continue stirring and bring slowly to the boil.

7   Cook over a low heat for 15 minutes. A few minutes before the rice is ready, add the white wine, mix well and then stir in the remaining butter. Cover the pan tightly with a lid, turn off the heat and leave to stand for 2 minutes. Heap the rice into a hot serving dish. Serve at once.

Rice with chicken and lobster

Preparation: 1 hour 25
  minutes

1 1.2-kg/2³/₄-lb roasting
  chicken
350 g/³/₄ lb fresh or tinned
  lobster meat
2 green peppers
2 medium onions
4 large ripe tomatoes
175 g/6 oz long-grain rice
225 ml/8 fl oz oil
6 tsp soy sauce
pepper

1   Skin and bone the chicken and cut into strips.

2   Dice the lobster flesh (drain well if tinned).

3   Pour 125 ml/4 fl oz of oil into a large, heavy-bottomed saucepan and sauté the strips of chicken; add the diced lobster and continue cooking over a low heat for up to 20 minutes.

4   Wash and dry the green peppers, remove the seeds and white membrane; peel the onions and chop these and the peppers coarsely. Dice the tomatoes and add to the peppers, onions and the remaining oil in another saucepan; cook over a high heat for a few minutes.

5   Sprinkle the rice into the saucepan with the vegetables and continue cooking, stirring constantly, for 5 minutes more.

6   Add the rice, tomato and pepper mixture to the pan containing the pieces of chicken and lobster.

7   Add the soy sauce and plenty of freshly ground pepper; stir well and add just enough warm water to cover the rice. Boil briskly for 10 minutes, until the rice is tender but still firm. Transfer to a preheated serving dish and serve with extra soy sauce.

Five-colour fried rice

3 dried Chinese mushrooms
50 g/2 oz cooked ham
100 g/3¹/₂ oz pork
1 leek
2 eggs
100 g/3¹/₂ oz prawns
salt
oil for frying

2 tsp soy sauce
pinch pepper
50 g/2 oz lard or cooking fat
800 g/1³/₄ lb precooked
    rice, (preferably boiled 24
    hours in advance)
3 tbsp peas, precooked

1   Soak the mushrooms in warm water for 20 minutes, remove the stems and cut the caps into 5-mm/¹/₄-in squares. Dice the ham and pork to the same size; chop the leek finely. Shell the prawns and chop into pieces 5-mm/¹/₄-in thick.

2   Beat the eggs and season with salt. Heat 1 tablespoon oil in a wok; pour in the eggs and scramble, then set aside on a plate.

3   Wipe the wok and heat 1 tablespoon fresh oil; stir-fry the mushrooms gently over a moderate heat until their full aroma is released.

4   Add the pork and stir-fry, stirring to keep the cubes from sticking to one another; when the pork has changed colour, add the prawns and the ham. Fry lightly.

5   Once the prawns have changed colour, if raw, or have heated through, if precooked, pour in 2 teaspoons soy sauce, trickling it down the inside of the wok; stir and turn, giving the soy sauce time to flavour the other ingredients, and then season with pepper. Remove ingredients from the wok and set aside.

6   Clean the wok, pour in 3 tablespoons oil and heat; stir-fry the leek to flavour the oil but do not allow it to brown.

7   Add the rice and stir-fry over a moderate heat, stirring and turning continuously, taking care not to crush the rice grains. Season with ¹/₂ teaspoon salt.

8   When the rice is well mixed and coated with oil, add the reserved ingredients and stir-fry; add the scrambled egg and peas and mix once more before serving.

Semolina gnocchi

Preparation: 1 hour (+ 2 hours for the semolina to stand)

¹/₂ litre/1 pint milk
80 g/3 oz butter
salt
175 g/6 oz fine semolina
50 g/2 oz grated Parmesan
15 g/¹/₂ oz grated Sbrinz or Pecorino

1   Heat the milk in a saucepan, add one third of the butter and a pinch of salt.

2   Bring to the boil then gradually stir in the semolina. Cook for 20 minutes, stirring frequently.

3   Remove from the heat and stir in 30 g/1 oz grated Parmesan.

4   Pour the semolina into a dampened shallow dish, spreading it out evenly to a thickness of about 5mm/ ¹/₄ in.

5   Leave to cool for 2 hours then cut into circles 4cm/ 1¹/₂ in in diameter.

6   Arrange the gnocchi slightly overlapping in a buttered ovenproof dish and sprinkle with the remaining Parmesan.

7   Melt the remaining butter and pour over the gnocchi.

8   Cover with the grated Sbrinz and transfer to a very hot preheated oven, at 200°C/400°F/mark 6 for about 10 minutes until lightly browned.

Gnocchi Parisian style

Preparation: 50 minutes

225 ml/8 fl oz water
125 g/4 oz butter
salt
200 g/7 oz flour
4 eggs
nutmeg
150 ml/5 fl oz Mornay
   sauce*

1 Bring the water and 80 g/
3 oz butter to the boil in a
high-sided saucepan. Add a
pinch of salt.

2 When the butter has
completely melted, remove
from the heat and gradually
add the flour, stirring
constantly. Leave to cool
slightly.

3 Beat in the eggs one at a
time and add a pinch of
nutmeg.

4 Spoon the mixture into a
piping bag with a 2.5cm/1-
in-diameter nozzle. Pipe
gnocchi 4 cm/1¹/₂ in long
into a saucepan of boiling
salted water and cook for 15
minutes. Drain.

5 Heat the remaining
butter in a small saucepan
until light brown. Pour over
the gnocchi.

6 Transfer the gnocchi to a
lightly buttered ovenproof
dish; cover with Mornay
sauce and place in a very
hot preheated oven at
200°C/400°F/mark 6 for 10
minutes until the top is
golden brown.

Meat couscous

Serves 8-10

Preparation: 2¹/₂ hours

1 1.2-1.4-kg/2³/₄-3-lb fresh
  chicken, boned and cut
  into pieces
1 1.4-1.5 kg/3-3¹/₂ lb mutton
  (neck and shoulder),
  boned and cut into cubes
200 g/7 oz chickpeas,
  presoaked and parboiled
8 ripe tomatoes
225 g/¹/₂ lb pumpkin or
  marrow flesh (rind and
  seeds removed)

6 medium onions, sliced
1 envelope saffron powder
  or pinch turmeric
50 g/2 oz sultanas
  (presoaked in warm
  water)
600 g/1¹/₄ lb coarse semolina
125 g/4 oz butter
2 cloves
pinch mixed spice
pinch chilli powder
salt and pepper

1   Bring 1³/₄ litres/3 pints water to a boil in a large saucepan. Rub the chicken and mutton with salt and pepper and add to the boiling water with the onions, chilli powder, mixed spice, cloves, a piece of butter and the chickpeas.

2   Pour the semolina onto a large shallow plate and sprinkle with a cup of salted water. Work it over so all is evenly moistened.

3   Continue to knead the semolina. If too damp, add a little more semolina.

4   Sieve the semolina once it has amalgamated into small pellets. Spread out on a clean tea towel. Dry in the oven, at 130°C/250°F/mark ¹/₂ with the door open.

5   Add the chopped tomatoes and pumpkin flesh to the ingredients that have been boiling.

6   Spread the teacloth with the semolina inside a metal colander. Fold over the edges and place over the boiling meat and vegetables. Cover tightly and steam for 30 minutes.

7   Turn the semolina onto a large plate and separate any pellets that have stuck together. Sprinkle with a little cold water, mix very gently and sprinkle again.

8   After about 2 hours, when the meat is tender, remove from heat and add the sultanas tied up in a cheesecloth; add the saffron or turmeric and return to the heat. Replace the semolina in the colander and steam for 5 more minutes. Spread on a heated serving platter, dot with butter and gradually sprinkle with the stock from the meat. Arrange the meat and vegetables on the semolina. Serve the remaining stock separately.

Fish couscous

Preparation: 2 hours 15
   minutes

1 kg/2¹/₄ lb assorted fish
   (hake, grey mullet,
   gurnard or other)
1 onion
1 clove garlic
1 large ripe tomato
300 ml/10 fl oz oil
1 tbsp chopped parsley
1 bay leaf
salt and pepper
175 g/6 oz couscous
pinch nutmeg
pinch cinnamon

1   Clean the fish, rinse well, and drain. Slice the onion finely. Chop the garlic. Peel the tomato, remove and discard the seeds, and chop coarsely.

2   Heat 200 ml/7 fl oz oil in a large saucepan. Add the garlic, chopped parsley, bay leaf and finely sliced onion, and brown for 2 minutes. Add the tomato.

3   Place the fish in the saucepan, with the largest on the bottom. Pour over 1½ litres/2½ pints water, season with salt and pepper, and simmer for 5 minutes.

4   Remove the fish and keep warm. Strain the stock and pour three quarters into the bottom of a couscous pan.

5   Place the couscous steamer on top of the pan. (In the absence of a special steamer use a colander lined with cheesecloth or foil.) Place the couscous inside, pour over the remaining oil, stir, and cover tightly to prevent steam escaping during cooking.

6   Place a weight on the lid and simmer gently for 20 minutes. During cooking the couscous will absorb the flavour of the fish stock.

7   Pour the couscous into a frying pan, stir in some of the reserved stock, and leave to stand for 1 hour. Add more stock as the couscous expands and absorbs the liquid, and stir.

8   Arrange the couscous on a warm serving dish and pour over the cooking juices. Season with pepper, nutmeg, and cinnamon. Add salt if necessary. Place the fish fillets on top.

Fish and Seafood

Hake Bulgarian style

Preparation: 40 minutes

2 hake, total weight 1 kg/
    2¼lb
salt and pepper
2 tbsp fresh dill
2 tbsp chopped parsley
6 tbsp brandy

1   Remove the scales from the fish; clean, rinse, and pat dry.

2   Sprinkle with salt and pepper.

3   Mix together the chopped dill and parsley.

4   Grill the fish for about 20 minutes, turning frequently.

5   Place the fish in a large frying pan and sprinkle with the chopped herbs.

6   Heat the brandy, pour over the fish, and flame. Serve at once.

Leghorn red mullet

Preparation: 1 hour

8 red mullet, total weight
    800 g/1¾ lb
20 g/¾ oz flour
6 tbsp oil
1 celery stalk
2 cloves garlic
400 g/14 oz ripe tomatoes
    (or tinned)
salt
black pepper
1 tbsp chopped parsley

1   Clean, rinse, and dry the fish and coat lightly in flour.

2   Heat 4 tbsp oil until very hot and fry the fish over a high heat for 3 minutes on each side. Drain and keep warm.

3   Finely chop the celery and garlic and fry gently in a large saucepan for 3 minutes in the remaining oil.

4   Add the peeled and chopped tomatoes, salt, and pepper and cook uncovered for 15 minutes.

5   Pass the tomato sauce through a vegetable mill or liquidize briefly.

6   Return the fish to the saucepan, cover with the tomato sauce, and reheat gently for 15 minutes.

7   Arrange the fish on a warm serving dish, cover with the sauce, and sprinkle with chopped parsley. Serve immediately.

Tempura

(Japanese mixed fry)

Preparation: 2 hours

1 small crawfish
16 prawns
1 sole
salt and pepper
4 tbsp soy sauce
4 tbsp saké (Japanese rice
   wine)
2 tsp sugar
1½ tbsp fresh horseradish
1 tsp powdered ginger
4 scallops
1 green pepper
1 carrot
225 g/8 oz green beans
2 eggs
150 g/5 oz flour
oil for deep frying

1   Remove the meat from the crawfish shell. Shell and clean the prawns, removing the heads.

2   Fillet the sole. Make a fish stock by placing the heads from the prawns, the head of the crawfish – the latter cut into four – and the bones and trimmings from the sole into a small saucepan with 2 ladles of water and a little salt. Simmer for 15 minutes and then boil rapidly to reduce.

3   Pour the stock through a strainer with a fine mesh and leave to cool. Add the soy sauce, saké, and sugar. Stir well and pour into four individual bowls. Before serving sprinkle with the grated horseradish and ginger.

4   Cut the fillets of sole into long strips; clean and slice the scallops. Cut the meat from the crawfish into slices.

5   Wash the vegetables. Dice the pepper and carrot; string the beans and leave whole.

6   Beat two egg yolks with a ladle of cold water in a bowl and work in the flour using a whisk.

7   Dip the pieces of fish and vegetables in the batter before frying.

8   Heat enough oil in a large cast-iron frying pan or wok and, keeping the temperature constant, deep fry the fish and vegetables in batches. Season with salt and pepper and serve very hot. Each person dips a selection of fried fish and vegetables into the soy sauce.

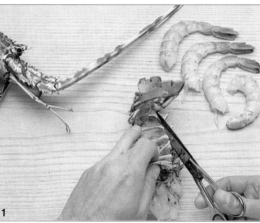

Tuna Charterhouse style

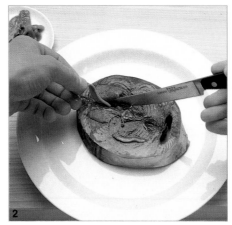

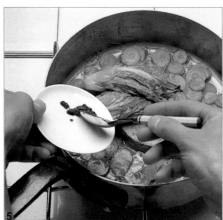

Preparation: 1 hour

4 tuna steaks
salt and pepper
1 lemon
4 anchovy fillets
1 onion
3 carrots
3 tbsp oil
4 lettuce hearts
1 bunch sorrel
200 ml/7 fl oz white wine

1   Place the tuna steaks in boiling salted water acidulated with the lemon juice and boil for 1 minute.

2   Drain and dry the tuna steaks. Make several incisions in each and insert the pieces of anchovy.

3   Finely slice the onion and cut the carrots into rounds. Pour the oil into a large saucepan, add the onion and carrots, season with salt and pepper, and fry for 4 minutes. Place the tuna steaks on top of the vegetables, cover and cook for 3 minutes. Add salt, turn the steaks, and cook for a further 3 minutes.

4   Cook the lettuce hearts in boiling salted water for 2 minutes.

5   Drain and squeeze the lettuce hearts and place on top of the tuna steaks. Rinse and dry the sorrel and place in the centre of the steaks. Cook for 4 minutes over a moderate heat.

6   Sprinkle with salt and pepper and white wine; cover and simmer for about 20 minutes. Serve each steak with a selection of the vegetables and garnish with a little fresh sorrel.

Conger eel Braganza style

Preparation: 1 hour

800 g/1³/₄ lb conger eel
6 tbsp oil
1 small onion
1 bay leaf
1 tbsp vinegar
salt and pepper
4 slices day-old bread
3 egg yolks
1 tbsp chopped parsley

1   Wash and dry the eel and cut into 5-cm/2-in slices.

2   Heat the oil in a saucepan, add the chopped onion, and fry gently for 5 minutes.

3   Add the eel, bay leaf, vinegar, 225 ml/8 fl oz water, salt, and pepper. Bring to the boil and simmer for 10 minutes.

4   Arrange the slices of day-old bread on a heated serving dish and place the drained pieces of eel on top. Keep warm. Reserve the cooking liquid.

5   Beat together the egg yolks and parsley.

6   Stir the cooking juices gradually into the beaten egg yolks and parsley and heat gently until thickened. Pour the sauce over the eel and serve at once.

Sea bass with orange sauce

Preparation: 40 minutes

1 800-g/1³/₄-lb sea bass
4 tbsp oil
50 g/2 oz flour
salt
40 g/1¹/₂ oz butter
200 ml/7 fl oz milk
3 oranges (preferably blood
  oranges)

1   Cut the sea bass into steaks 2 cm/³/₄ in thick.

2   Heat the oil in a frying pan. Coat the steaks lightly in flour and fry for 10 minutes over a medium heat, turning after 5 minutes. Season with salt, drain, and keep warm.

3   Melt the butter in a clean saucepan, stir in the flour and cook the roux for 2 minutes.

4   Stir in the milk gradually and cook for 5 minutes.

5   Squeeze two oranges.

6   Add the orange juice to the white sauce and cook for a further 5 minutes, stirring constantly. Add salt to taste.

7   Pour the sauce over the fish steaks and cook gently for another 5 minutes.

8   Wash the remaining orange and, without peeling, cut it into fine slices. Cut each slice in half and use for garnish.

Stuffed grey mullet

Preparation: 1 hour

$^{1}/_{2}$ onion
$^{1}/_{2}$ green pepper
1 large tomato
75 g/3 oz butter
1 1-kg/2$^{1}/_{4}$-lb grey mullet
1 tbsp chopped parsley
salt and pepper
6 tbsp white wine
fresh dill

1   Finely chop the onion and pepper.

2   Peel the tomato, remove the seeds, and chop coarsely.

3   Melt half the butter in a frying pan and fry the onion, pepper and tomato for 5 minutes.

4   Remove the scales from the grey mullet. Make an opening in the side, clean, rinse well under running water and wipe dry.

5   Stuff the fish with the onion, pepper, tomato, and chopped parsley. Season with salt and pepper.

6   Sew up the opening carefully with kitchen thread.

7   Place the fish in a buttered roasting tin. Pour over the wine and the remaining melted butter.

8   Bake in a preheated oven at 200°C/400°F/mark 6 for 20 minutes, basting frequently with the juices and sprinkling with chopped dill after 10 minutes.

Sea bream with olives

Preparation: 40 minutes

1 1.2-kg/2³/₄-lb sea bream
4 tbsp oil
24 black olives, stoned
salt and pepper
200 ml/7 fl oz white wine
4 sprigs rosemary

1   Remove the scales, clean, and rinse the sea bream.

2   Pour the oil into a large frying pan and fry the fish gently for 3 minutes on each side.

3   Add the stoned olives, season with salt, and pour in the wine. Cook for a further 15 minutes.

4   Add the sprigs of rosemary, sprinkle generously with pepper, and cook for another 5 minutes. Serve immediately.

John Dory with vegetables

Preparation: 45 minutes

1 1-kg/2¹/₄-lb John Dory
   (sole or turbot may be
   substituted)
1¹/₂ tbsp flour
6 tbsp oil
salt
4 artichokes
sprig rosemary
juice of ¹/₂ lemon
225 ml/8 fl oz white wine
1 tbsp chopped parsley
black pepper
25 g/1 oz butter

1   Clean and rinse the fish
and cut into four. Wipe dry
and coat lightly with flour.

2   Heat the oil in a large
frying pan and, when hot,
place the pieces of fish in
side by side.

3   Fry for 3 minutes on
each side, then sprinkle with
salt.

4   Trim the artichokes,
discarding the tough outer
leaves. Slice finely and add
to the frying pan together
with the rosemary. Season
with salt.

5   Pour in the lemon juice,
add the wine, and cook for
about 15 minutes.

6   Sprinkle with the finely
chopped parsley and black
pepper and cook,
uncovered, for 3 minutes.

7   Arrange the artichokes
on a heated serving dish and
place the fish on top.

8   Make a beurre manié by
blending the butter and flour
together well. Add a small
quantity at a time and stir
into the sauce to thicken.
Pour over the fish.

Fried hake maître d'hôtel

Preparation: 40 minutes
  (+ 2 hours for the *maître
  d'hôtel* butter to chill)

8 small hake
2 eggs
flour for coating fish
175 g/6 oz fine breadcrumbs
4 tbsp white wine vinegar
oil for frying
salt and pepper

For the maître d'hôtel
  butter:
125 g/4 oz butter
juice of ¹/₂ lemon
1-2 tbsp finely chopped
  parsley

106

1   Work the butter until soft and then mix in the chopped parsley, followed by the lemon juice.

2   Roll the butter in waxed paper or foil into a large sausage-shape (about 3 cm/1¼ in in diameter). Chill in the refrigerator for at least 2 hours.

3   Gut the fish, wash well and dry.

4   Pour the vinegar into a bowl and dilute with an equal amount of cold water. Use a clean cloth wrapped around three fingers and dipped in the acidulated water to wipe the cavities of the fish; do not rinse off.

5   Coat the fish in flour and dip into the egg beaten with a little salt.

6   Roll in the breadcrumbs, pressing lightly so that the whole fish is coated.

7   Heat plenty of oil until very hot in a large frying pan and lower the fish carefully into it.

8   Fry the fish until they are well browned, spooning hot oil over them occasionally. Remove and drain on kitchen paper. Slice the *maître d'hôtel* butter and place a round of butter on each fish. Garnish with sprigs of parsley and serve with steamed potatoes.

Skate au beurre noir

Preparation: 1 hour
  (+ 2 hours for soaking the
  skate)

1.2 kg/2³/₄ lb wing of skate
salt and pepper
1 onion
2 carrots
4 sprigs parsley
4 tbsp wine vinegar
10 peppercorns
1 bay leaf
1 tbsp chopped parsley
1¹/₂ tbsp capers
75 g/3 oz butter

1   Buy ready-cleaned skate or have it cleaned and skinned by the fishmonger. Wash under cold running water and leave to soak in salted water for 2 hours.

2   Slice the onion and carrots.

3   Cut the skate into four.

4   Place the skate in a wide frying pan with the onion, carrot, parsley, 2 tablespoons of wine vinegar, salt, peppercorns, and bay leaf. Cover with cold water, bring to the boil, and simmer very gently for 15 minutes.

5   Drain the skate and arrange on a serving dish.

6   Sprinkle with salt, pepper, chopped parsley and crushed capers. Keep warm.

7   Melt the butter in a small saucepan and heat until it turns golden brown. Take care not to burn it. Pour the butter over the skate. Return the saucepan to the heat, warm the remaining wine vinegar, and pour over the fish. Serve immediately with boiled new potatoes topped with butter and parsley.

Turbot with prawn sauce

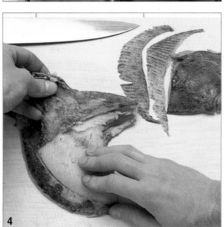

Preparation: 1 hour

3 uncooked Dublin Bay
   prawns
$^1/_2$ tbsp flour
salt
75 g/3 oz butter
pinch mace
Cayenne pepper
1 1.2-kg/2$^3/_4$-lb turbot
200 ml/7 fl oz milk
$^1/_2$ lemon
pepper
1 tbsp chopped parsley

1   Boil the Dublin Bay
prawns for 3 minutes in
5 cm/2 in of water. Shell
them, return the shells to the
water, and cook for a further
15 minutes. Strain the stock
and reduce by boiling
vigorously.

2   Mix the flour with
100 ml/4 fl oz of the stock
and add a pinch of salt. Add
the butter in pieces and
cook, stirring constantly, for
3 minutes.

3   Add the meat from the
prawns cut into pieces, a
pinch of mace and Cayenne
pepper. Stir for 1 minute
until the sauce thickens.

4   Clean the turbot: cut off
the head and fins and
remove the skin and entrails.

5   Cover with 200 ml/7 fl
oz water and the milk, then
add the lemon juice. Season
with salt and pepper and
cook for about 15 minutes.

6   Drain the turbot, place
on a warm serving dish, and
sprinkle with chopped
parsley. Serve with boiled
potatoes and carrots and
serve the prawn sauce
separately in a sauce boat.

Salt cod Vicenza style

Preparation: 2 hours (+ 2
   days for soaking the salt
   cod)

800 g/1³/₄ lb salt cod
2 onions
1 clove garlic
2 anchovies
1 tbsp parsley
salt and pepper
225 ml/8 fl oz oil
125 g/4 oz grated Parmesan
¹/₂ litre/1 pint milk

1   Beat the salt cod with a wooden rolling pin, then leave to soak in cold water for 2 days, changing the water frequently.

2   Cut the salt cod into strips 5 cm/2 in wide; open them out and remove the bones.

3   Skin each piece.

4   Finely chop the onions, garlic, anchovies and parsley. Season with salt and pepper. Heat half the oil in a saucepan and fry the ingredients for 5 minutes before adding the Parmesan. Stir well.

5   Use the filling to sandwich the pieces of salt cod together.

6   Heat the remaining oil in a frying pan, add the salt cod and any remaining filling.

7   Heat for 2 minutes, then pour in the milk.

8   Cook very gently for 1½ hours, shaking the frying pan occasionally to prevent the salt cod from sticking. This dish is traditionally served with slices of fried polenta.

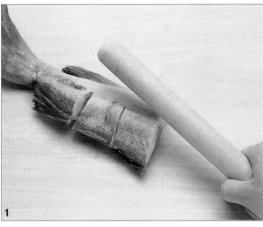

Steamed fish Cantonese style

1 whole very fresh non-oily,
  white fleshed fish, such as
  bass, carp, mullet, etc,
  weighing approximately
  600 g/1¼ lb
2-3 dried Chinese
  mushrooms, presoaked
2 slices root ginger
2 slices ham
1 leek
1 tbsp rice wine
few drops of sesame oil
2 tbsp soy sauce

1 Always use the freshest fish for this recipe; gut and clean.

2 With a sharp knife remove the scales from the fish; wash it well in cold running water inside and out and pat dry.

3 Soak the Chinese mushrooms in water for 20 minutes, then drain. Remove the stems and slice the caps into thin strips about 3 mm/⅛ in wide.

4 Pound one slice of ginger with the blunt edge of the cleaver; cut the second slice into thin strips.

5 Shred the ham and cut the leek into two pieces, each 10 cm/4 in long.

6 Place the pounded slice of ginger in the cavity of the fish; lay the fish on its side in an ovenproof dish with one piece of leek under its head and the other under its tail. Sprinkle the shredded ginger, ham and mushrooms over the top of the fish.

7 Moisten the fish with 1 tablespoon rice wine and a few drops of sesame oil for flavour; place the dish in the bamboo steamer, which should already be full of steam.

8 Steam the fish over rapidly boiling water for 15 to 20 minutes without opening the steamer; when the fish is cooked, remove the slice of ginger from the inside of the fish. Place the fish on a heated serving dish and sprinkle with the rice wine while still hot.

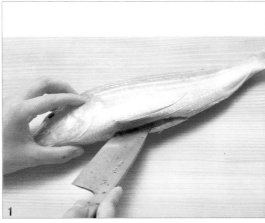

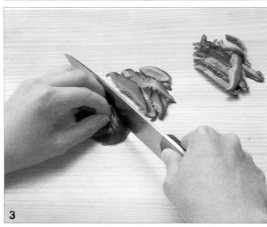

Pompano en papillote

Preparation: 1 hour

2 pompano (turbot, salmon,
   trout or bass may be
   substituted), total weight
   1 kg/2¹/₄ lb
400 ml/14 fl oz fumet*
300 ml/10 fl oz dry white
   wine
75 g/3 oz butter
225 g/8 oz prawns
1 tbsp chopped parsley
2 onions
40 g/1¹/₂ oz flour
Cayenne pepper
salt
1-2 tbsp single cream
225 g/8 oz cooked crabmeat

1   Clean and fillet the fish. Rinse and pat dry.

2   Place the fillets in a frying pan with half the fumet, the wine, and a little butter. Bring to a simmer and heat gently for 5 minutes.

3   Peel the prawns and remove the central black vein. Wash and pat dry with kitchen paper.

4   Melt half the butter in another frying pan, add the prawns, and cook for 3 minutes. Sprinkle with chopped parsley.

5   Melt the remaining butter in a saucepan, add the chopped onions, and fry for 5 minutes; add the flour and stir constantly with a whisk for 1 minute.

6   Add the remaining fumet; bring to the boil, lower the heat, and simmer for 3 minutes. Stir in a little Cayenne pepper, salt, and the cream.

7   Cut out 8 foil heart shapes and butter 4 of them. Place a fillet of fish, a quarter of the prawns, and a quarter of the crabmeat on each.

8   Spoon over a little of the sauce and cover with a piece of foil. Seal the edges well. Place the papillotes on a baking tray in a preheated oven at 200°C/400°F/mark 6 for 8 minutes. Serve immediately.

Sole à la meunière

Preparation: 20 minutes

4 sole, total weight 1 kg/
   2¹⁄₄lb
65 g/2¹⁄₂ oz butter
1 tbsp flour
salt
1 tbsp lemon juice
1 tbsp chopped parsley

1   Clean the sole; remove the skin from the dark side and gently scrape the white side.

2   Melt half the butter in a large frying pan. Dip the sole in flour and shake off the excess.

3   Gently fry the sole in the butter for 6 to 7 minutes, turning once with a fish slice, and season with salt.

4   When the sole are golden brown, transfer to a heated serving dish and sprinkle with a few drops of lemon juice and finely chopped parsley.

5   In the same frying pan heat the remaining butter until golden brown and foaming. Pour over the sole and serve immediately.

Fillets of sole à la normande

Preparation: 50 minutes
(+ 2 hours for cleaning
the mussels)

450 g/1 lb mussels
125 g/4 oz prawns
300 ml/10 fl oz fumet*
125 g/4 oz mushrooms
50 g/2 oz butter
4 fillets of sole (or 450 g/
  1 lb)
200 ml/7 fl oz white wine
salt and pepper
25 g/1 oz flour
3 egg yolks
juice of 1 lemon

1   Clean the mussels (*see* page 147) and heat them in a covered saucepan for 3 minutes. Remove from the shells; strain and reserve the liquor. Heat the prawns for 4 minutes in 3 tablespoons fumet. Peel them, place the shells in the fumet, and simmer for 5 minutes. Strain the fumet.

2   Wash and slice the mushrooms. Heat for 10 minutes in 15 g/½ oz butter.

3   Place the fillets in a buttered ovenproof dish with the wine and 6 tablespoons fumet. Season. Cover with buttered foil and bake at 170°C/325°F/mark 3 for 8 minutes.

4   Pour the liquor into the remaining fumet and reduce over a high heat.

5   Melt 25 g/1 oz butter, stir in the flour and cook for 1 minute. Add the fumet gradually and cook for 3 minutes. Beat the egg yolks and stir into the sauce. Add the remaining butter and lemon juice.

6   Transfer the fillets to another casserole dish. Surround with mushrooms, mussels and prawns; cover with sauce and place in the oven preheated to 200°C/400°F/mark 6 for 5 minutes.

Crawfish Sardinian style

Preparation: 1 hour

2 450-g/1-lb crawfish
2 onions
4 tbsp oil
1 tsp mustard
1 tsp vinegar
salt and pepper
2 medium tomatoes

1   Tie the crawfish with string, plunge them into boiling salted water, and cook for 10 minutes.

2   Finely slice the onions and leave to soak in a bowl of salted water for 10 minutes.

3   When the crawfish have cooled cut the tails in half.

4   Using a teaspoon carefully remove the creamy substance from the head and place in a bowl.

5   Add to it 3 tablespoons oil, the mustard, vinegar, salt and pepper, and stir vigorously.

6   Remove the meat from the tail and cut into slices.

7   Drain the onions, pour over the remaining oil, and chop the tomatoes into small pieces. Sprinkle with salt.

8   Arrange a layer of onion on each plate and place the slices of crawfish on top. Pour over the sauce and sprinkle with the pieces of tomato.

Lobster Newburg

Preparation: 40 minutes

1 1-kg/2¹/₄-lb lobster or
    crawfish
salt and pepper
50 g/2 oz butter
6 tbsp Madeira or Marsala
¹/₂ litre/1 pint cream
5 egg yolks
pinch Cayenne pepper
225 g/8 oz long-grain rice
2 tbsp chopped parsley

1   Tie the lobster or
crawfish with string and
cook in a large pan of boiling
salted water for about 15
minutes.

2   Leave to cool slightly
then remove the meat from
the tail and cut into chunks.

3   Melt the butter in a frying
pan and heat the pieces of
fish for 2 minutes.

4   Pour in the Madeira and
350 ml/10 fl oz cream. Bring
to the boil, lower the heat,
and simmer for 2 minutes.

5   Mix the egg yolks with
the remaining cream and a
few tablespoons of the
Madeira sauce.

6   Add the Madeira mixture
to the frying pan stirring
constantly. Heat gently until
the sauce thickens but do
not allow to boil.

7   Season with a pinch of
Cayenne pepper, salt and
black pepper.

8   Cook for a further 2 to 3
minutes. Serve on a bed of
steamed rice and sprinkle
with chopped parsley.

Lobster à l'américaine

Preparation: 1 hour

2 450-g/1-lb cooked lobsters
salt and pepper
6 tbsp oil
¹/₂ onion
2 shallots
1 clove garlic
6 tbsp brandy
250 ml/9 fl oz white wine
4 ripe tomatoes
225 ml/5 fl oz fumet*
pinch Cayenne pepper
1 tbsp tomato purée
2 tbsp parsley
1 tbsp tarragon
25 g/1 oz butter

1   Cut the lobsters in half lengthwise, removing and reserving the coral and liver, and cut each half tail into three and the head into two. Remove the claws. Season with salt and pepper. Heat the oil in a frying pan, add the lobster pieces, including the claws, and fry over a high heat, stirring until they turn red. Cook for a further 4 minutes.

2   Remove the pieces of lobster and add the chopped onions, shallots, and garlic. Fry gently for 8 minutes, return the lobster to the frying pan, pour over the brandy and flame. Stir in the wine, chopped tomatoes, fumet, and Cayenne pepper. Cover and simmer for 5 minutes.

3   Remove the meat from the claws and tails and keep warm. Pound the shells and heads and return to the sauce. Add the tomato purée and cook for 5 minutes. Sieve the sauce and reduce over a high heat. Stir in the coral and liver, the parsley and tarragon, and the pieces of lobster. Simmer for 1 minute, stir in the butter and heat for a further minute before serving.

Crab Venetian style

Preparation: 45 minutes

4 spider crabs, total weight
   1 kg/2¼ lb
salt and pepper
1 bunch parsley
3 tbsp oil
1 lemon

1 Plunge the crabs into boiling salted water and cook for 6 minutes.

2 Drain the crabs and leave to cool; pull away the legs and crack open with a nutcracker. Remove the flesh and chop finely.

3 Turn the crab over and pull the body away from the shell. Using a teaspoon, scrape out the eggs and set aside.

4 Remove all the meat (discard the grey stomach sac and ''dead men's fingers'') from the shell.

5 Finely chop the meat and add to the chopped flesh from the legs. Reserve the shells.

6 Finely chop the parsley.

7 Spoon the chopped meat back into the reserved shells and place a spoonful of the eggs in the centre of each. Sprinkle with chopped parsley and season with oil, lemon juice, salt and pepper.

Crab Louis

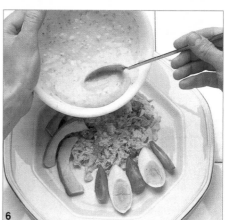

Preparation: 1 hour

1 1.2-kg/2¾-lb crab
salt
1 lettuce
2 tomatoes
2 hard-boiled eggs
1 small avocado
15 tbsp mayonnaise
2 tbsp chopped onion
3 tbsp chilli sauce
1 tbsp Worcestershire sauce
Cayenne pepper
2 tbsp chopped parsley
1 tbsp lemon juice
6 tbsp whipped cream

1   Plunge the crab into boiling salted water and cook for 20 minutes until it turns bright red. Allow to cool slightly before extracting the meat from the body, claws, and legs (see page 125).

2   Cut the lettuce into strips, rinse and drain. Arrange on a serving dish with the crabmeat on top.

3   Cut the tomatoes, eggs, and avocado into wedges and arrange around the crabmeat.

4   In a bowl blend together the mayonnaise, onions, chilli sauce, Worcestershire sauce, Cayenne pepper, chopped parsley and lemon juice.

5   Fold in the whipped cream.

6   Spoon the sauce over the crabmeat and serve.

Potted crab

Preparation: 1 hour

1 1.2-kg/2³/₄-lb crab
salt
³/₄ teaspoon Cayenne
    pepper
¹/₄ teaspoon nutmeg
pinch mace
1 lemon
50 g/2 oz butter
2 tbsp clarified butter*

1 Plunge the crab into boiling salted water and cook for 20 minutes.

2 Break off the claws and legs. Pull off and discard the grey feathery gills ("dead men's fingers") and the grey stomach sac. Spoon out the meat and separate the white from the creamier, darker part. Crack the claws and extract the meat.

3 Place the meat in two separate bowls. Season with salt, Cayenne pepper, nutmeg, mace and lemon juice.

4 Spoon into 4 ramekins in alternate layers of light and dark meat.

5 Melt the butter and divide equally between the ramekins.

6 Place the ramekins in a bain-marie; bake in a preheated oven at 170°C/325°F/mark 3 for 15 minutes.

7 Allow to cool before turning out.

8 Pour a little clarified butter over each one and serve with toasted bread.

Dublin Bay prawns in tomato and white wine sauce

Preparation: 30 minutes

20 uncooked Dublin Bay
   prawns
3 tbsp oil
2 cloves garlic
salt and black pepper
350 g/12 oz tomatoes
200 ml/7 fl oz white wine
1 tbsp chopped parsley

1 Rinse the Dublin Bay prawns and with a sharp knife cut each one in half down the back.

2 Heat the oil in a large frying pan.

3 Coarsely chop the garlic and fry gently in the oil for 2 minutes.

4 Remove the garlic with a slotted spoon.

5 Place the prawns side by side on their backs in the flavoured oil.

6 Season with salt and plenty of freshly ground black pepper, then spoon over the coarsely chopped tomatoes. Cook for 2 minutes.

7 Pour in the white wine, cover, and simmer for 10 minutes. Sprinkle the prawns with chopped parsley and continue cooking uncovered for a further 2 minutes. Season with more black pepper and serve at once.

Chilli fried prawns

15 uncooked Dublin Bay
   prawns
oil for frying
1 tsp finely chopped garlic
1 tbsp chopped leek
1 tsp finely chopped ginger
1 tbsp rice wine
1 tsp cornflour

For the sauce:
125 ml/4 fl oz chicken stock
6 tbsp tomato ketchup
1 tsp salt
$^1/_2$ tbsp sugar
1 tsp Tabasco sauce

1   Rinse and drain the prawns; remove the heads by bending them over and inward, towards the tails. Remove the shells.

2   Slit the prawns down their backs with a sharp knife, stopping short of the second to last joint nearest the tail and being careful not to cut through or the prawns will separate into two halves.

3   Remove the black vein of the prawns using a cocktail stick.

4   Rinse the prawns and dry with kitchen paper. Strip off the tail flippers with scissors.

5   Spread the prawns on kitchen paper and remove excess moisture by pressing carefully with the flat of a knife blade.

6   Heat plenty of oil in a wok or deep-fryer to 180°C/340°F/mark 4 and lower the prawns carefully into the hot oil; stir with chopsticks or tongs, remove, and drain. Chop the garlic, leek and ginger.

7   Heat 2 tablespoons oil in the wok and stir-fry the garlic, leek and ginger; when these start to release their aroma, add the prawns.

8   Pour in the rice wine and the sauce ingredients; stir-fry to make sure the prawns are well flavoured, and then stir in the cornflour dissolved in 2 teaspoons water to thicken the sauce so that it will coat the prawns.

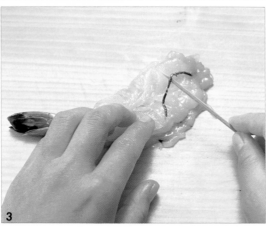

Curried prawns

Preparation: 1 hour 10 minutes

1 kg/1-2¼ lb uncooked prawns
salt
½ onion
1 tomato
1 clove garlic
4 tbsp oil
3 tbsp plain yoghurt
½ tsp powdered ginger
½ tsp chilli pepper
1 tsp turmeric
½ tsp cumin
1 tbsp wine vinegar
½ tsp sugar
125 g/4 oz long-grain rice

1   Blanch the prawns in boiling salted water for 3 minutes and then remove the shells.

2   Chop the onion. Blanch and peel the tomato and remove the seeds.

3   In a blender or food processor mix together all the ingredients, with the exception of the onion and prawns, until the sauce is well blended.

4   Heat the oil in a frying pan and cook the prawns for 5 minutes. Remove with a slotted spoon and drain.

5   Fry the onion until tender in the same pan in the remaining oil for 5 minutes.

6   Add the sauce from the blender to the saucepan and bring to the boil.

7   Lower the heat and simmer gently for 8 minutes, stirring occasionally, until the sauce has reduced slightly.

8   Add the prawns and cook for 3 minutes. Serve on a bed of steamed rice and garnish with chopped parsley.

Prawns à la créole

Preparation: 40 minutes

800 g/1³/₄ lb cooked prawns
2 small onions
1 celery stalk
1 small green pepper
1 clove garlic
350 g/12 oz ripe tomatoes
175 g/6 oz long-grain rice
1¹/₂ tbsp oil
50 g/2 oz butter
¹/₂ bay leaf
pinch thyme
1 tsp paprika
2 drops Tabasco
salt

1   Shell and rinse the cooked prawns.

2   Chop the onions and celery. Dice the green pepper and chop the garlic. Remove the seeds from the tomatoes and chop.

3   Steam the rice for 16 minutes.

4   Heat the oil and butter in a frying pan. Add the onion, celery and pepper and fry for 5 minutes. Add the garlic and cook for 1 minute.

5   Add the bay leaf, thyme, paprika, Tabasco and tomatoes. Season with salt.

6   Bring to the boil, lower the heat, and simmer for 15 minutes.

7   Stir in the prawns and cook for another 4 minutes. Serve with the steamed rice.

135

Oysters Florentine

Preparation: 1 hour

24 fresh oysters
400 g/14 oz fresh spinach
    (or use frozen)
1 large shallot
175 ml/6 fl oz dry white wine
400 ml/14 fl oz fish stock*
50 g/2 oz butter
25 g/1 oz flour
175 ml/6 fl oz cream
2 egg yolks
1 tsp oil
1 tsp lemon juice
salt
white pepper

1   Scrub the shells and with an oyster knife or other very strong knife, prize the shell open and remove the oyster.

2   Pour the liquor from the shells through a fine sieve into a bowl.

3   Chop the shallot finely and sauté in half the butter until pale golden brown. Add the oysters and the dry white wine and simmer, stirring and turning gently, for 2-3 minutes. Season with a little salt and freshly ground white pepper.

Remove the oysters with a slotted spoon and keep warm.

4   Melt the remaining butter in another saucepan. Stir in the flour and gradually mix in the hot fish stock. Stir until the sauce has thickened and then add the oyster liquor, the lemon juice and a little more salt if necessary. Finally, beat the egg yolks with the cream and gradually stir into the sauce. Remove from heat.

5   Rinse the spinach very well and heat gently for 5 minutes with no added water and with a pinch of salt. Refresh under cold water, chop coarsely and warm in the wine and juices left over from cooking the oysters.

6   Place the carefully cleaned oyster shells on a lightly greased baking tray and fill each shell with spinach; top with an oyster. Coat with a spoonful of sauce and bake in a preheated oven at 200°C/400°F/mark 6 for 20 minutes.

Chilled oyster soup

Preparation: 30 minutes
  (+ 2 hours for chilling)

800 g/1³/₄ lb oysters
50 g/2 oz butter
2 slices bacon
1 onion
50 g/2 oz flour
1 litre/1³/₄ pints milk
2 tbsp sherry
175 m/6 fl oz single cream
2 tbsp chopped parsley
salt
pepper
¹/₂ tsp paprika

1   Prize open the shells over a bowl using a strong, short-bladed knife. Remove the oysters and reserve the liquid.

2   Melt the butter and gently fry the finely chopped bacon and onion for 5 minutes.

3   Sprinkle in the flour and cook for 1 minute, stirring constantly.

4   Add the very hot milk and the reserved oyster liquid. Boil for 3 minutes until thickened.

5   Remove from the heat and add the sherry and cream, stirring thoroughly until well blended.

6   Add the oysters and 1 tablespoon parsley and cook for 5 minutes over a moderate heat. Season with salt and pepper.

7   Leave to cool, then refrigerate for 2 hours. Serve in individual bowls, and sprinkle with paprika and chopped parsley.

Creamed oysters

Preparation: 30 minutes

32 oysters
300 ml/¹/₂ pint milk
265 ml/9 fl oz single cream
pinch celery seeds
20 g/³/₄ oz butter
salt and pepper
pinch paprika

1   Prize open the oysters with a short bladed-knife and cut them from the shell. Strain the liquor into a small bowl and reserve.

2   Heat the milk and cream in a small saucepan; add the celery seeds and 2 tablespoons of the oyster liquor and boil for 5 minutes. Strain through a fine sieve.

3   Melt the butter in a separate saucepan. Add the oysters with 2 tablespoons of the reserved liquor and cook gently for 3 minutes. Remove from the heat.

4   Add the milk and cream, season with salt and pepper, and cook for a further 2 minutes.

5   Arrange the oysters in heated bowls and cover with the creamy sauce.

6   Sprinkle with paprika and serve at once.

Scallops in white wine

Preparation: 40 minutes
 (+ 1 hour for cleaning the
 scallops)

16 scallops
2 leeks
50 g/2 oz butter
salt
225 ml/8 fl oz Riesling (or
 other medium dry white
 wine)
pepper

1   Leave the scallops under cold running water for 1 hour. Prize the shells open and cut out the scallop, discarding the black gristly part around the cushion.

2   Cut the white part of the leeks into strips.

3   Melt the butter and fry the leeks briefly. Sprinkle with salt and pour in the wine.

4   Cook gently for 5 minutes. Add the scallops and cook, covered for a further 5 minutes.

5   Remove the scallops and leeks and keep warm.

6   Reduce the sauce over a medium heat. Place a layer of leeks on each plate; top with scallops, sprinkle with pepper, and cover with sauce.

Sea date soup

Preparation: 1 hour
   (+ 2 hours for cleaning
   sea dates)

1 kg/2^1/$_4$ lb sea dates
6 tbsp oil
2 cloves garlic
1^1/$_2$ tbsp chopped parsley
pinch Cayenne pepper
220 ml/7 fl oz single cream
1 tsp meat extract
225 g/8 oz tinned tomatoes
225 ml/8 fl oz white wine
salt

If sea dates are unavailable,
substitute mussels.

1 Rinse the sea dates, preferably under running water, for 2 hours, to remove all traces of sand.

2 Drain them and heat for 4 minutes in a covered frying pan until they open. Remove from their shells.

3 Reserve the cooking liquor and strain through a fine sieve.

4 Pour the oil into another frying pan and gently heat the finely chopped garlic.

5 Add 1 tablespoon parsley, the Cayenne pepper, cream, meat extract, tomatoes, wine and reserved liquor.

6 Cook for 15 minutes, then strain through a fine sieve into a saucepan.

7 Add the sea dates and heat for 2 minutes. Adjust the seasoning. Sprinkle with the remaining chopped parsley and serve with slices of hot fried or toasted bread.

Mediterranean fish stew

Serves 8

Preparation: 1 hour
    30 minutes

4 medium-sized onions
6 tbsp oil
450 g/1 lb fish trimmings
    (tails, heads, bones etc.)
5 large ripe tomatoes
450 g/1 lb shellfish (fresh,
    preferably uncooked)
1-1$^{1}/_{2}$ kg/2-3$^{1}/_{2}$ lb assorted
    fresh fish (monkfish,
    turbot, sole, mussels,
    hake, whiting, etc.)

175 ml/6 fl oz dry white wine
1 clove garlic
1 bouquet garni
1 packet saffron threads (or
    pinch turmeric)
salt and pepper

*For the accompanying
sauce:*
3 egg yolks
1 clove garlic
225 ml/8 fl oz good-quality
    olive oil
salt and pepper

To prepare the sauce:
Place the egg yolks in a fairly
large bowl and beat together
with a crushed garlic clove;
continue stirring briskly in
the same direction, adding
the oil a few drops at a time.
Season. The sauce can be
turned an attractive orange
colour by adding a little of
the saffron-coloured fish
stock.

1   Peel the onions, slice very thinly and heat gently in the oil in a large, heavy-bottomed saucepan

2   Continue cooking, stirring frequently, until the onions are golden brown.

3   Add the fish trimmings and stir for a few minutes over a fairly high heat; pour in the dry white wine, season with a little salt and freshly ground pepper and bring to the boil. Pour in enough water to completely cover and bring back to the boil.

4   Blanch, peel and remove the seeds from the tomatoes; chop coarsely and add to the pan. Crush the garlic and add, together with the bouquet garni; simmer for 20 minutes.

5   Strain the mixture through a fine sieve and return to a clean saucepan.

6   Soak the saffron threads in 6 tablespoons of hot water and add to the strained fish stock or, alternatively, the turmeric. Bring again to the boil.

7   Lower the larger pieces of the fish into the hot stock and after about 10 minutes add the smaller fillets and the shellfish. Continue simmering until all the fish is cooked; do not stir, simply shake the saucepan from time to time to prevent the fish sticking to the bottom. Adjust the seasoning. Serve this fish stew piping hot with toasted garlic bread sprinkled with Parmesan. Pass the sauce around separately in a bowl or sauceboat.

Manhattan clam chowder

Preparation: 1 hour 20
    minutes (+ 2 hours for
    cleaning the clams)

1 kg/2¼ lb clams
175 g/6 oz fatty bacon
1 medium onion
1 carrot
1 celery stalk
225 g/8 oz tinned tomatoes
1 bay leaf
pinch thyme
salt and pepper
2 small potatoes

1   Rinse the clams,
preferably under running
water, for 2 hours, to
remove all traces of sand.

2   Place the clams in a
saucepan; cover and cook
for 3 minutes or until the
shells open. Strain and
reserve the cooking liquid.

3   Remove the clams from
their shells.

4   Chop the fatty bacon
and fry for 1 minute. Add
the chopped onion, carrot
and celery and cook for 5
minutes.

5   Add the tomatoes, bay
leaf, thyme, and reserved
cooking liquid from the
clams. Season with salt and
pepper and cook for 6
minutes.

6   Add 4 ladles of water
and bring to the boil. Lower
the heat, add the peeled and
diced potatoes, and simmer
for 20 minutes.

7   Add the clams and heat
gently for 2 minutes before
serving.

Moules marinière

Preparation: 20 minutes
 (+ 2 hours for cleaning
 the mussels)

2 kg/4¹/₂ lb mussels
1 onion
3 shallots
1 clove garlic
40 g/1¹/₂ oz butter
250 ml/9 fl oz white wine
¹/₂ bay leaf
pinch thyme
black pepper
2 tbsp chopped parsley

1   Scrub the mussels
thoroughly, removing the
beard-like threads, and
leave under running water
for 2 hours to rinse through
of sand.

2   Chop the onion, shallots
and garlic.

3   Melt the butter in a large
saucepan and gently fry the
onion and shallots until
tender. Add the garlic and
cook for a further 1 minute.

4   Add the wine, bay leaf,
thyme and black pepper and
cook for 2 minutes.

5   Add the mussels and
cook for 5 minutes, shaking
the saucepan occasionally,
until all the shells have
opened. Discard any which
have not.

6   Sprinkle with parsley
and serve the mussels in
bowls with the cooking
liquid.

Cuttlefish with peas

Preparation: 40 minutes

800 g/1³/₄ lb cuttlefish (or
   squid)
¹/₂ onion
6 tbsp white wine
salt and pepper
225 g/8 oz tomatoes
400 g/14 oz shelled peas
¹/₂ tbsp sugar
1 sprig rosemary

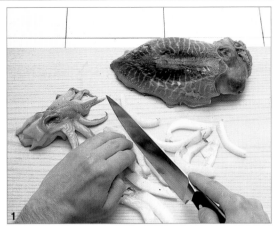

1   Remove the central bone of the cuttlefish by pressing in the end of the sac-like body and pulling from the opposite end. The head will pull away, together with the bone, the ink sac and entrails. Reserve the tentacles and discard the rest. Rinse and dry the cuttlefish, rubbing off the purplish skin; cut in half lengthwise and chop into strips 5 cm/2 in long.

2   Finely chop the onion and brown in the oil.

3   After 4 minutes add the strips of cuttlefish and chopped tentacles.

4   Cook for 5 minutes, then pour in the wine. Season with salt, cover and cook for a further 5 minutes.

5   Add the skinned seeded, and chopped tomatoes and cook, uncovered, over a high heat for 5 minutes.

6   Add the peas and sugar.

7   Cook for a further 15 minutes. Add the rosemary, adjust the seasoning and sprinkle with pepper. Reduce the sauce by boiling vigorously for 1 minute, then serve.

Stuffed squid

Preparation: 1 hour

8 squid, total weight
    800 g/1³/₄ lb
8 black olives, stoned
1 tbsp capers
2 tbsp chopped parsley
2 drops Tabasco
2 drops Worcestershire
    sauce
1 tbsp breadcrumbs
6 tbsp oil
1 clove garlic
2 tomatoes
salt and black pepper
pinch oregano

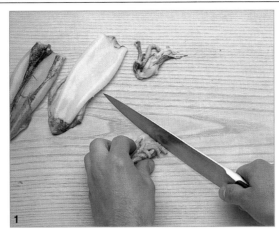

1   Cut off the tentacles, remove and discard the ink sac attached to the head. Pull out and discard the central transparent "pen" and rub off the purplish outer skin.

2   Chop the tentacles.

3   Finely chop the olives, capers, and parsley.

4   Place all the chopped ingredients, including the tentacles, in a bowl and add 2 drops each of Tabasco and Worcestershire sauce, breadcrumbs and 2 tablespoons oil. Mix well.

5   Stuff each squid with a little filling and carefully sew the ends with kitchen thread.

6   Finely chop the garlic and skinned and seeded tomatoes.

7   Pour the remaining oil into a large frying pan. Gently fry the chopped garlic over a very low heat for 2 minutes. Add the chopped tomatoes and cook for a further 2 minutes.

8   Add the stuffed squid and a little salt. Cover and simmer for 20 minutes. Sprinkle with oregano and black pepper and cook for 3 minutes. Serve immediately.

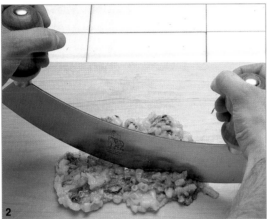

Coulibiac of salmon

Preparation: 1 hour
  30 minutes

225 g/8 oz fresh salmon
125 g/4 oz butter
salt and pepper
$^1/_2$ tsp paprika
$^1/_2$ tsp dried dill
6 tbsp white wine
$^1/_2$ lemon
3 shallots
175 g/6 oz rice
450 ml/16 fl oz chicken stock
3 eggs (2 hard-boiled)
1 tbsp chopped parsley
175 g/6 oz mushrooms
2 tbsp chopped chives
400 g/14 oz puff pastry
soured cream (optional)

1   Cut the salmon into chunks and place in a buttered roasting pan. Sprinkle with salt, paprika and dill. Pour the wine and lemon juice over the salmon. Cover with foil and place in a preheated oven 180°C/350°F/mark 4 for 15 minutes.

2   Melt a quarter of the butter in a small saucepan and brown 2 chopped shallots for 1 minute. Add the rice, stir for 1 minute, then pour in the stock and cook for 15 minutes.

3   Stir into the rice two chopped hard-boiled eggs, the parsley, salt and pepper.

4   Melt 2 tablespoons butter in a frying pan; add the remaining finely chopped shallot and the sliced mushrooms and cook for 6 minutes. Sprinkle with salt and the chopped chives.

5   Roll out the pastry into a rectangle 5 mm/$^{1}/_{4}$ in thick. Arrange alternate layers of rice, salmon and mushrooms in the centre, leaving a generous amount of pastry to fold over.

6   Brush down one side of the pastry with beaten egg. Fold over the other side to enclose the filling and press down gently to seal the edge.

7   Place the salmon roll on a buttered baking tray. Cut decorative leaves with any remaining pastry. Leave two holes for the steam to escape, then brush the roll with beaten egg. Leave to stand for 20 to 30 minutes. Bake at 200°C/400°F/mark 6 for 10 minutes, then lower to 190°C/375°F/mark 5 for 30 minutes.

8   Leave to cool for 15 minutes, then pour melted butter into the holes. Serve with more melted butter or soured cream.

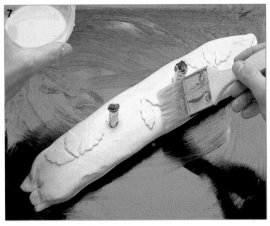

Gravlax

Preparation: 1 hour
  (+ 1 day for the salmon to stand)

bunch dill
5 peppercorns
1 800-g/1³/₄-lb fresh salmon
40 g/1¹/₂ oz sugar
1 tbsp sea salt
2 tbsp Dijon mustard
2 tbsp white wine vinegar
6 tbsp oil
1 lemon

1   Rinse and dry the dill and crush the peppercorns.

2   Remove the head and cut the salmon in half. Remove the backbone using a sharp knife and leave the skin intact. Rinse and dry well.

3   In a small bowl mix together 2 tablespoons sugar, the salt and the crushed peppercorns.

4   Place half the salmon, skin side down, in a long shallow dish and sprinkle with 1 tablespoon chopped dill and the mixture of salt, sugar and pepper. Place the other half, skin side up, on top.

5   Wrap in foil, cover with another plate and place a 3-kg/6¹/₂-lb weight on top. Refrigerate for at least 24 hours. Turn after 12 hours, spooning over the juices.

6   Place the salmon on a chopping board and slice off thin pieces diagonally.

7   Prepare the sauce: mix together the mustard, remaining sugar and vinegar. Blend in the oil gradually. Add the remaining chopped dill.

8   Arrange the slices on a serving dish, cover with the sauce and garnish with lemon wedges. Serve any remaining sauce separately.

Anguilles au vert

Preparation: 1 hour

125 g/4 oz fresh sorrel
2 tbsp chopped parsley
6 leaves tarragon
3 leaves sage
2 eels, total weight
   1 kg/2¼ lb
50 g/2 oz butter
salt and pepper
300 ml/10 fl oz white wine
2 egg yolks
1 tbsp lemon juice

1   Rinse and finely chop the sorrel. Chop the parsley, tarragon and sage.

2   Rinse and skin the eels. Divide in half lengthwise, remove the backbone, and cut into 6-cm/2½-in pieces.

3   Brown the pieces of eel in the butter for 5 minutes. Add the sorrel and other chopped herbs. Season with salt and pepper and pour in the wine.

4   Bring to the boil, lower the heat and simmer for 15 minutes. Transfer the eel pieces to a serving dish.

5   Beat the egg yolks with a little of the cooking liquid, then pour into the saucepan.

6   Heat gently for 3 minutes, stirring constantly, until the sauce thickens. Add the lemon juice.

7   Pour the sauce over the eel and leave to cool before serving.

Eel pie

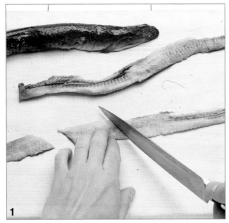

Preparation: 1 hour
   20 minutes

1 1-kg/2¹/₄-lb eel
75 g/3 oz butter
1 large shallot
200 ml/7 fl oz Marsala
pinch nutmeg
1 tbsp chopped parsley
salt and pepper
50 g/2 oz flour
juice of ¹/₂ lemon
2 hard-boiled eggs
50 g/2 oz frozen shortcrust
   pastry

1 Rinse and skin the eel and cut into 5-cm/2-in pieces.

2 Melt 25 g/1 oz butter in a frying pan and brown the finely chopped shallot. Add the Marsala, nutmeg, parsley, 200 ml/7 fl oz water, salt and pepper, and cook for 4 minutes.

3 Place the pieces of eel in a large buttered ovenproof pan.

4 Melt the remaining butter and stir in the flour. Cook gently for 1 minute.

5 Stir in the mixture from the frying pan and the lemon juice. Bring to the boil stirring constantly, and cook for 3 minutes.

6 Pour the sauce over the eel. Place the slices of hard-boiled egg on top and cover with the rolled-out pastry. Bake in a preheated oven at 200°C/450°F/mark 6 for 10 minutes, then lower to 180°C/350°F/mark 4 for 30 minutes.

Carp Jewish style

Preparation: 1 hour 15
   minutes (+ 2 hours for
   chilling)

1 1.2-kg/2³/₄-lb carp
150 g/5 oz blanched
   almonds
1 onion
2 shallots
8 tbsp oil
1¹/₂ tbsp flour
1 tbsp sugar
300 ml/10 fl oz fish stock*
50 g/2 oz sultanas
1 bouquet garni
1 clove garlic
salt and pepper
1 tbsp chopped parsley

1 Clean and rinse the carp.

2 Chop the almonds into thin slivers.

3 Finely chop the onion and shallots.

4 Pour half the oil into a frying pan. Add the chopped onion and shallots and fry for 2 minutes.

5 Stir in the flour and sugar and cook for 2 minutes before adding the fish stock, almonds, and sultanas.

6 Place the carp in a fish kettle with the bouquet garni and crushed garlic. Pour over the sauce.

7 Heat gently for a few minutes before seasoning with salt and pepper. Cook over a moderate heat for a further 30 minutes.

8 Drain the carp and place on a serving dish. Reduce the cooking liquid by boiling vigorously. Discard the bouquet garni and add the remaining oil, stirring with a balloon whisk. Adjust the seasoning and allow to cool before pouring the sauce over the fish. Chill for at least 2 hours and sprinkle with chopped parsley before serving.

Stuffed pike

Preparation: 1 hour
   15 minutes (+ 45 minutes
   for soaking the prunes)

15 prunes
1 1-kg/2¼-lb pike
125 g/4 oz long-grain rice
salt and pepper
3 hard-boiled eggs
50 g/2 oz butter
dry breadcrumbs

1   Soak the prunes in warm water for 45 minutes. Drain them, stone; chop half of them coarsely. Reserve the remaining prunes.

2   Remove the scales, clean, rinse and dry the pike. Sprinkle with salt.

3   Cook the rice in boiling salted water for 12 to 15 minutes or until tender. Chop the hard-boiled eggs.

4   Stuff the pike with a mixture of rice, egg, the chopped prunes, salt and pepper and half the butter.

5   Sew up the cavity of the fish with kitchen thread.

6   Coat the fish in the breadcrumbs.

7   Place in a buttered roasting tin and dot with the remaining butter.

8   Bake in a preheated oven at 150°C/300°F/mark 2 for 15 minutes, then raise the heat to 200°C/400°F/mark 6 for a further 10 minutes or until cooked. Remove the thread. Serve on a bed of rice and garnish with the remaining prunes.

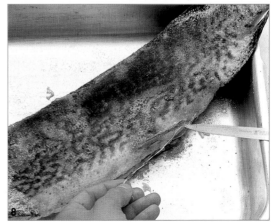

Stuffed trout with almonds

Preparation: 1 hour
    15 minutes

4 boned whole trout
2 eggs
80 g/3 oz soft breadcrumbs
milk
2 onions
2 spring onions or shallots
225 ml/8 fl oz dry white wine
15 g/¹/₂ oz butter
few tbsps fine breadcrumbs
50 g/2 oz slivered almonds
6 tbsp oil
salt and pepper

1   Hard-boil an egg, place under cold running water, shell and mash with a fork. Moisten the soft breadcrumbs with a little milk, squeeze well and then mix with the mashed hard-boiled egg.

2   Sauté the finely chopped onion and spring onions or shallots gently in 2 tablespoons oil, season with salt and pepper and then blend with the breadcrumbs and egg mixture. Stir in the remaining egg.

3   Fill the cavity of each trout with a quarter of this stuffing.

4   Sew up the sides of the trout with oil and coat with fine breadcrumbs.

5   Brush the trout with oil and coat with fine breadcrumbs.

6   Arrange the trout in a lightly greased ovenproof dish and pour in the white wine.

7   Sprinkle the slivered almonds over the fish.

8   Grease a piece of foil and place on top of the trout, buttered side down. Bake in a preheated oven 180°C/350°F/mark 4 for about 30 minutes, spooning some of the wine and cooking juices over the fish occasionally to keep moist. Remove the foil after twenty minutes to allow almonds to brown. Serve immediately.

Meat, Poultry and Game

Veal and mushrooms Istanbul

Preparation: 1 hour

800 g/1³/₄ lb veal escalopes,
   thinly sliced
5 tbsp oil
juice of ¹/₂ lemon
1 large onion
175 ml/6 fl oz dry white wine
300 ml/¹/₂ pint light stock
275 g/10 oz mushrooms
1 tbsp tomato purée
25 g/1 oz bacon
6 tbsp cream
paprika
salt and pepper
cornflour (optional)

166

1 Clean the mushrooms and place in a bowl of water mixed with the lemon juice to prevent them from discolouring. Dry and slice just before cooking.

2 Chop the onions and the bacon; sauté in a saucepan in 2 tablespoons oil. As soon as the onion starts to turn brown, add the sliced mushrooms. Stir and fry gently over a moderate heat for about 10 minutes. Season with a pinch of salt and a little freshly ground pepper. Remove from heat.

3 Pound the veal slices with a meat mallet dipped in cold water (this can be done between two layers of clingfilm). Trim off any fat and cut into strips.

4 Dust the strips of veal with flour, place in a sieve and shake to get rid of excess flour.

5 Sauté the strips in the remaining oil over a fairly high heat; turn so that they colour evenly and sprinkle with a pinch of salt. Using a slotted spoon, transfer the veal strips to a heated dish, cover and keep warm.

6 Stir the wine into the juices in the pan, stirring with a wooden spoon until the wine has almost completely evaporated.

7 Stir in the tomato purée and the light stock (preferably veal stock); then dribble in the cream while stirring.

8 Add the sautéed vegetables and bacon to the sauce, then the veal strips. Stir until every strip of veal is coated with sauce and sprinkle with a generous pinch of paprika. Cook for 10-15 minutes until the sauce has reduced slightly. Thicken with a little cornflour dissolved in cold water if desired. Serve with pilaf rice*.

Classic veal fricassée

Preparation: 2 hours

1 kg/2¼ lb veal, cut into
  small cubes
1½ litres/3½ pints light stock
1 small carrot, 1 leek and 1
  onion stuck with a clove
1 bouquet garni
125 g/4 oz skinned baby
  onions
175 g/6 oz mushrooms

50 g/2 oz butter
50 g/2 oz flour
3 egg yolks
6 tbsp cream
juice of ¼ lemon
grated nutmeg
1 tbsp finely chopped
  parsley
salt and pepper

1   Place the cubed veal in a large saucepan and pour in enough strained stock to cover by at least 2 cm/³/₄ in. Bring to a gentle boil and continue cooking while skimming off the scum from the top.

2   Add the carrot, leek, onion and bouquet garni and continue to simmer gently for 1 hour 50 minutes.

3   Cook the onions separately for about 40 minutes, adding 25 g/1 oz butter, 2 tablespoons water and a pinch of salt so that they are lightly glazed when done.

4   Clean, trim and thinly slice the mushrooms and boil for about 10 minutes in 125 ml/4 fl oz water.

5   Strain the veal and reserve the cooking stock; place the veal in another saucepan and add the onions and strained mushrooms; keep warm.

6   Melt the remaining butter, stir in the flour then gradually stir in the hot stock from the veal.

7   Cook the sauce over a low heat for 15 minutes, stirring with a wooden spoon and removing any scum that collects during cooking. Beat the egg yolks with the cream and a few drops of lemon juice; dribble this into the veal stock sauce, stirring continuously and briskly so that the egg mixture will not curdle. Add a pinch of nutmeg and bring almost to the boil.

8   Pour the sauce through a sieve onto the veal, onions and mushrooms and stir the veal in the sauce over a low heat; remove from heat as soon as it starts to boil and transfer to a deep, warm serving dish. Sprinkle with parsley and serve.

Roast fillet of beef
with wine sauce

Preparation: 1 hour
   10 minutes

1 kg/2^1/$_4$ lb beef fillet
700 ml/1^1/$_4$ pints beef stock
225 g/^{1}/$_2$ lb cubed lean beef
1 onion
1 carrot
1 celery stalk
1 tsp tomato purée
175 ml/6 fl oz dry white wine
50 g/2 oz cornflour
8 tbsp oil
salt and pepper
watercress

1   If not already done, tie the meat with string so that it will hold its shape while cooking.

2   Sprinkle generously with salt and freshly ground pepper.

3   Heat 4 tablespoons oil in a heavy sauté pan or frying pan over a fairly high heat and add the beef; cook for 15 minutes to seal the flavour and brown evenly all over. Remove the meat from the oil.

4   Wrap the beef in foil and then wrap in a towel. Keep warm (this way the meat will not dry out or toughen).

5   Trim, wash and prepare the vegetables. Chop the onion coarsely, dice the carrot and celery; sauté in the remaining 4 tablespoons of oil.

6   Transfer the vegetables to a second heavy-bottomed pan, add the cubed beef; stir and sauté for a few minutes before seasoning with salt and pepper. Add the wine and when this has almost completely evaporated sprinkle in the cornflour.

7   Stir in the tomato purée mixed with the hot stock; simmer for 40 minutes, skimming off any scum from the surface.

8   Strain off the cooking liquid into a saucepan; blend the diced beef and the vegetables in a food processor. Pour this mixture back into the cooking liquid and bring to the boil. Remove the wrappings and string from the fillet, cut into fairly thick slices and garnish with watercress. Serve the sauce very hot, passing it round separately.

Beef olives

Preparation: 1 hour
  50 minutes

8 fairly thin pieces of beef
  (e.g. sirloin steak, cut
  against the grain, or
  silverside cut into cross-
  grained slices), each
  trimmed to measure
  about 20 × 20 cm/8 × 8 in
1 large onion
2 carrots

1 celery stalk
4 large ripe tomatoes
¹/₂ litre/1 pint tomato juice
200 ml/7 fl oz red wine
2 tbsp oil
40 g/1¹/₂ oz butter
25 g/1 oz beurre manié
  (15 g/¹/₂ oz butter beaten
  with 15 g/¹/₂ oz flour)
2 tbsp milk
salt and pepper

For the stuffing:
225 g/8 oz minced pork
225 g/8 oz finely chopped or
  minced lean beef
pinch thyme
pinch powdered bay leaf
few ground fennel seeds
pinch ground coriander
salt and pepper

1 Cover the slices of beef with clingfilm and beat gently with a meat mallet.

2 Prepare the filling: place minced pork and beef in a bowl and add the seasonings and herbs; mix well until all the ingredients have combined in a smooth paste.

3 Place two flattened pieces of beef so that they slightly overlap, place a quarter of the stuffing in the middle and roll up, tying firmly with string.

4 Heat 25g/1oz butter in a frying pan with the oil. When it is very hot add the beef olives and brown on all sides. Season with salt and pepper, remove from frying pan and keep warm.

5 Clean and trim the carrots and celery and peel the onion before chopping into small pieces. Melt the remaining butter in a large saucepan, add the vegetables and sweat gently over a low heat.

6 Add the beef olives, pour in the wine and, as soon as it has evaporated, add the peeled, seeded and diced tomatoes and the tomato juice; stir and then leave to simmer gently for about 30 minutes. Remove the beef olives from the saucepan and keep hot on a heated serving platter.

7 Add the milk to the sauce and beat in with a whisk or hand-held beater.

8 Add the beurre manié. Season with a little salt and freshly ground pepper. Push the sauce through a sieve (or blend in an electric blender or food processor) and pour over the beef olives, some of which can be sliced and ready to serve.

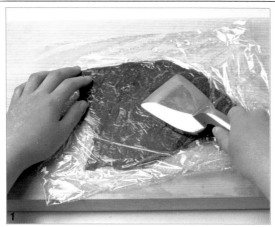

Argentine braised beef

Serves 6

Preparation: 2 hours
   50 minutes

1.4 kg/3 lb topside or
   silverside, cut into
   2.5 cm/1-in cubes
oil for browning
8 tbsp oil
2 large onions
2 green peppers
5 large ripe tomatoes
1 celery stalk
3 medium potatoes
275 g/10 oz pumpkin (skin
   and seeds removed)

2 small apples
225 g/8 oz cooked
   sweetcorn (fresh or tinned)
150 g/5 oz grapes
1 bouquet garni
300 ml/10 fl oz dry white wine
350 ml/12 fl oz stock
225 g/8 oz rice
3 peppercorns
1 clove garlic
salt
Cayenne pepper

This dish is spectacular
when served in a pumpkin.
Prepare the pumpkin by
slicing off the top, scooping
out all the seeds and
washing the inside; heat for
15 minutes in a hot oven.
Alternatively, serve the beef
in a rustic-looking deep
earthenware dish.

1 Brown the beef in 3 tablespoons of *very* hot oil in a large heavy-bottomed saucepan or enamel pot.

2 Sauté the sliced onions, the crushed clove of garlic and the peppers (seeds and pith removed and coarsely chopped) in the remaining oil over a gentle heat, using an earthenware or cast iron pot or frying pan. Add the chopped tomatoes.

3 When the vegetables have cooked through, transfer them with their juices to the pan containing the meat. While stirring, add the chopped celery and the bouquet garni. Season with salt, Cayenne pepper and the peppercorns.

4 Add the white wine a little at a time. When this is considerably reduced, pour in the hot stock and stir. Cover and cook over a low heat for 1 hour 15 minutes, stirring at frequent intervals.

5 While the beef and vegetables are simmering, peel and dice the potatoes, apples and pumpkin. Stir into the meat and vegetable mixture when it has cooked for the length of time given above. Continue cooking for a further 30 minutes.

6 Stir in the cooked, drained sweetcorn.

7 While the beef is braising cook the rice in plenty of salted boiling water; when it is tender, drain and then stir into the beef together with the grapes. Adjust the seasoning and cook for a few minutes longer. Serve immediately in a large, heated earthenware dish or, for a better effect, in a large pumpkin.

Marinated roast beef

Preparation: 2 hours
    50 minutes (+ 2 days for
    marinating the beef)

1 kg/2¼ lb topside or
    silverside
5 tbsp oil
few tbsp plain flour
1 medium onion
1 carrot
1 celery stalk
1 clove garlic
pinch freshly grated fresh
    ginger
1 small carton yoghurt
salt and pepper

For the marinade:
1 onion
2 shallots
1 carrot
450 ml/16 fl oz dry red wine
4 tbsp red wine vinegar
225 ml/8 fl oz water
1 bay leaf
few cumin seeds
thyme
salt
5 peppercorns

To prepare the marinade:
Wash, peel and finely slice
the onion, shallots and
carrot and place in a large
pot with the other
ingredients. Bring to a gentle
boil, stirring from time to
time; lower the heat and
simmer gently for 10
minutes. Cool to room
temperature.

1   Prepare the marinade following the instructions opposite. Immerse beef in the cooled marinade. Cover and leave in the refrigerator for two days, turning the beef several times.

2   After two days, take the beef out of the marinade and dry with kitchen towel. Set marinade aside. Season a few tablespoons of flour with salt and freshly ground pepper and flour the meat. Heat the oil in a large, heavy-bottomed fireproof saucepan or enamel pot and brown the beef all over; when well coloured, remove from pot and set aside.

3   In the same pot, sauté the finely sliced onion, carrot, celery and chopped garlic very gently for 5 minutes, stirring frequently.

4   Return the beef to the pot, pour the reserved marinade over it, add the grated fresh ginger and bring slowly to the boil.

5   As soon as the marinade starts to boil, turn down the heat, cover and simmer very slowly for $2^{1}/_{2}$ hours; use two wooden spatulas or tongs to turn the beef frequently so that it cooks evenly; whisk a tablespoon of yoghurt into the cooking liquid whenever the meat is turned.

6   When the beef is done, take out and allow to cool to room temperature. Strain the cooking liquid through a fine sieve, return to the pot and reheat.

7   Slice the cooked meat, place in the strained sauce and allow to heat over a very low heat. Arrange the slices on a heated serving platter, cover with a little of the sauce and pass around the rest of the sauce separately.

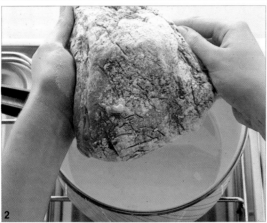

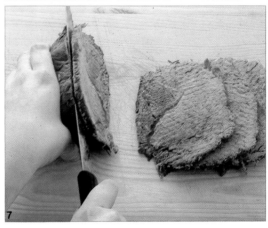

Carpetbag steaks

 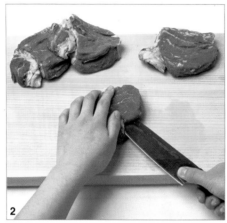 

Preparation: 1 hour

4 fillet, rump or porterhouse
   steaks
25 g/1 oz butter
16 fresh oysters
salt and pepper

For the sauce:
2 finely chopped shallots
4 ripe tomatoes
600 ml/1 pint stock made
   with a stock cube
6 tbsp port
40 g/1$^{1}/_{2}$ oz butter
25 g/1 oz beurre manié
   (15 g/$^{1}/_{2}$ oz flour worked
   into 15 g/$^{1}/_{2}$ oz softened
   butter)
salt and pepper

1   Cover the steaks with
clingfilm and pound with a
meat mallet.

2   Make an incision in one
side of each steak.

3   Push two oysters into
each steak and secure with a
cocktail stick.

4   *To prepare the sauce:*
Melt the butter in a
saucepan, add the shallots
and sauté until golden
brown.

5   Pour in the port and
cook until it has almost
completely evaporated.

6   Add the peeled, seeded
and roughly chopped
tomatoes, the remaining
oysters, also chopped, and
the stock; season. Let the
sauce simmer and reduce
before adding the beurre
manié, stirring the mixture
as the butter melts and
releases the flour into the
sauce to thicken it. While the
sauce is reducing fry the
steaks in the very hot butter,
seasoning them. Make sure
the steaks and their contents
are warmed through without
overcooking. Transfer the
steaks to a hot serving dish
and pour the sauce over
each one.

New England boiled beef and chicken

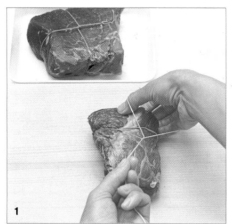

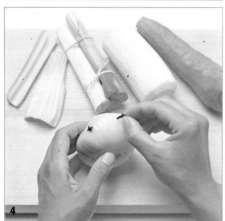

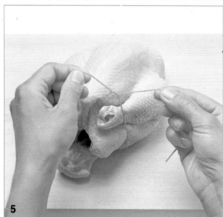

Serves 8

Preparation: 2 hours
    30 minutes

1 kg/2¼ lb topside
800 g/1¾ lb silverside
1 1-kg/2¼-lb chicken
1 small cabbage
1 onion
1 leek
2 carrots
2 celery stalks
1 clove garlic
1 turnip
2 cloves
salt

1   Tie the two cuts of beef together firmly with string.

2   Place the meat in a large pot with 3¼ litres/5½ pints water and a generous pinch of coarse salt; bring to the boil. Use a ladle to skim off the scum on the surface. Lower the heat and simmer over a very low heat for at least 1 hour.

3   Wash the cabbage; remove the hard stalk and strip off the leaves. Place the leaves in groups of four, one on top of the other; roll up each pile and tie with string.

4   Wash the leek, cut in half lengthwise and tie at top and bottom. Peel the turnip and the onion; stud the onion with the two cloves. Scrape the carrots, wash the celery stalks and cut into 7-10 cm/3-4 in lengths.

5   Wash and dry the chicken and truss with string.

6   Add the vegetables and chicken to the pot containing the beef, cover with foil or a tight-fitting lid and bring to the boil. Lower heat and simmer for 1 hour 15 minutes. Remove strings from chicken and vegetables. Serve each person with a selection of carved meats and some of the vegetables.

Jamaican loin of pork

Preparation: 1 hour
   30 minutes

1 kg/2¼ lb boneless loin of
   pork
6 tbsp oil
2 onions
2 cloves garlic
4 large ripe tomatoes
1 bouquet garni
1 cinnamon stick
175 ml/6 fl oz dry white wine
generous pinch grated
   nutmeg
few drops Tabasco sauce
salt and pepper

The original Jamaican recipe
calls for a garnish of sliced
bananas sautéed in butter
and seasoned with salt and
pepper, which adds a further
dimension to the flavour and
gives the dish a more
authentic, exotic touch.

1 Tie the boned loin of pork securely so that it will keep its shape as it cooks; sprinkle with a little salt and freshly ground pepper, brown well on each side in the oil in a large, heavy-bottomed casserole or enamel pot.

2 When the pork is golden brown all over, transfer to a stainless steel plate, cover and place over a saucepan of boiling water to keep the meat warm.

3 Sauté the finely chopped onions in the oil used to brown the meat; fry very gently until transparent but do not brown; place the loin of pork on top of the onions, sprinkle with the finely chopped garlic. Blanch and peel the tomatoes, cut in quarters and remove the seeds; add to the pork. Sprinkle the grated nutmeg into the casserole and crumble in the cinnamon stick; add the bouquet garni and 2 or 3 drops of Tabasco sauce.

4 Season with a little more salt and freshly ground pepper, pour in the dry white wine, cover and bring to a gentle boil over a fairly low heat. Place in a preheated oven at 200°C/400°F/mark 6 for 1 hour, basting frequently.

5 Remove the pork from the casserole, leaving it at room temperature to cool. Pour the cooking liquid through a fine sieve.

6 When the pork has cooled, remove the string and carve into slices. Pour a little of the strained juices into a shallow serving dish, arrange the pork slices in the dish, slightly overlapping one another, and cover with the remaining strained juices. Cover with foil and return to the oven for 10-15 minutes at 180°C/350°F/mark 4.

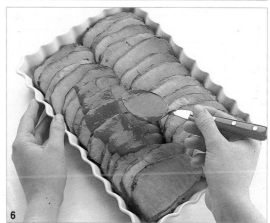

Pork chops with figs

Preparation: 1 hour

12 small pork chops
4 tbsp oil
175 ml/6 fl oz dry white wine
2 gherkins
2 finely chopped shallots
4 tbsp gravy (made with half
   a stock cube dissolved
   with 15 g/¹/₂ oz butter into
   1 tbsp white wine and 3
   tbsp water)
4 tinned figs (drained, syrup
   reserved)

juice of ¹/₂ lemon
¹/₂ tbsp tarragon
1 tsp of syrup from the
   tinned figs
6 tbsp cream
1 tbsp chopped parsley
1 tbsp plain flour
50 g/2 oz butter
salt and pepper

The contrast between the
sharp taste of the gherkins
and the smoothness of the
cream complements the
sweetness of the figs and
gives this dish a very
unusual sweet-and-sour
flavour.

1   Season the pork chops with a little salt and freshly ground pepper.

2   Heat the oil in a large frying pan and fry the pork on both sides; pour in the dry white wine and continue cooking until the wine has completely evaporated; remove the pork chops from the frying pan and keep warm.

3   Melt the butter in the frying pan, stir in the flour with a wooden spoon, making sure there are no lumps.

4   Add the cream, the gravy mixture and the finely chopped gherkins and shallots.

5   Continue stirring and add the figs and the teaspoon of syrup.

6   Sprinkle the chopped tarragon and the lemon juice into the sauce and simmer for a few minutes over a moderate heat to allow the sauce to reduce and thicken. Arrange the pork chops on a heated serving plate or directly onto the dinner plates, cover with sauce and sprinkle with the finely chopped parsley.

Pork chops in lemon sauce

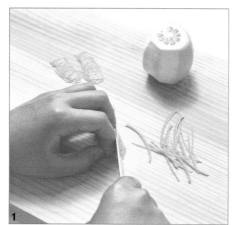

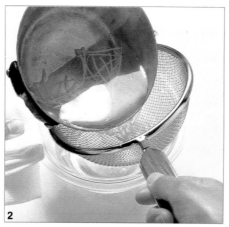

Preparation: 1 hour
20 minutes

8 pork chops
50 g/2 oz butter
salt and pepper

For the sauce:
2 lemons
600 ml/1 pint stock
175 ml/6 fl oz dry white wine
1 tbsp tomato purée
beurre manié (made with
15 g/½ oz butter and
15 g/½ oz flour)
25 g/1 oz butter
salt and pepper

1   Remove the peel of the lemons and cut into julienne strips; reserve the peeled lemons.

2   Place the julienne strips in a saucepan, cover with cold water, blanch for 2 minutes, then drain.

3   Heat the butter in a frying pan and fry the pork chops until they colour on both sides; season. When the pork is cooked through, take up and keep warm.

4   To prepare the sauce: add the wine and the stock to the cooking juices and heat until it has considerably reduced.

5   Stir in the tomato purée, remove from heat and mix in the beurre manié; return to the heat and stir constantly.

6   Add the strips of lemon peel and the whole lemon segments (pith and membrane removed). Season. Simmer gently for 15 minutes. Pour the sauce over the pork chops on the serving dish or individual plates. Serve with mashed potatoes, puréed carrots and a purée of peas (piped decoratively using a fluted nozzle and a piping bag); garnish with sprigs of watercress.

Thrice-cooked pork

Preparation: 4 hours

900 g/2 lb pork belly in one
  piece
1 leek
1 piece root ginger, finely
  chopped
oil for frying
1 star anise
1/2 tbsp cornflour

For the sauce:
4 tbsp soy sauce
1 tbsp sugar
1 tbsp rice wine or dry
  sherry
6 tbsp of the liquid in which
  the pork has been cooked

188

1 Bring plenty of water to a boil in a large saucepan; place the pork belly in the boiling water for a few minutes; remove and place in a fresh saucepan of boiling water together with a whole leek and the ginger. Cover and cook for approximately 35 minutes.

2 Mix the sauce ingredients.

3 When the pork is cooked, cool slightly, drain, and dry with kitchen paper. Heat plenty of oil to 180°C/350°F/mark 4 and fry the pork until it is well coloured all over.

4 Remove the pork and immediately rinse in very cold water; when cold enough to handle, slice into pieces about 5 mm/¼ in thick.

5 Place fat side down, in a heatproof dish; add the star anise and the sauce, sprinkling it evenly over the meat.

6 Place the dish in a bamboo steamer, over boiling water producing plenty of steam; cook over a moderate heat for about 2 hours, topping up the boiling water with hot water whenever needed to avoid burning the steamer.

7 Remove the dish from the steamer and cool; place in the refrigerator and remove the layer of fat which will form on the surface. Return the dish to the steamer and cook for a further 1 to 2 hours or until the pork is very tender. Transfer to a hot serving dish.

8 Pour the juices which have been produced during cooking into a saucepan, bring to the boil, and then stir in the cornflour dissolved in 1 tablespoon cold water. Cook briefly and then pour over the pork.

Sweet and sour pork

Preparation: 30 minutes

350 g/³/₄ lb leg of pork
   (boned)
1 red chilli pepper
2 leeks
1 tsp finely chopped garlic
¹/₂ small pineapple
4 green peppers
2 tsp cornflour
1 egg
cornflour as required
oil for frying
1 tbsp rice wine or dry
   sherry

For the sauce:
5 tbsp vinegar
1 tbsp soy sauce
3 tbsp sugar
1 tbsp tomato ketchup
2 tbsp Worcestershire sauce
¹/₂ tsp salt

1 Cut the pork into slices about 1 cm/¹/₂ in thick and pound each piece lightly on both sides with the blunt edge of the cleaver to tenderise; then cut into bite-size portions.

2 Remove the seeds from the chilli pepper and cut it into rings about 5 mm/¹/₄ in thick. Slice the leeks into 1-cm/¹/₂-in lengths, and chop the garlic very finely.

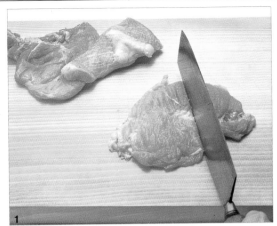

3 Drain the pineapple and chop; slice the green peppers and cut into portions the same size as the pork.

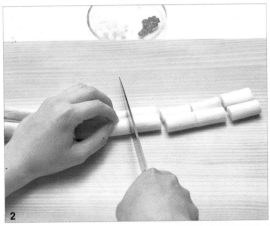

4 Mix the sauce ingredients together. In a separate small bowl or cup dissolve 2 teaspoons cornflour in 3 teaspoons cold water.

5 Dip the pork in the beaten egg and then coat with cornflour. Heat the oil over a medium heat in a wok and fry the pork until it is cooked through. Set aside.

6 Heat 2 tablespoons oil in the wok and stir-fry the garlic; as soon as this releases its aroma, add the leeks followed by the peppers.

7 When the peppers are tender, add the chilli pepper, the pineapple, and the pork and stir-fry, mixing and turning all the ingredients briskly: moisten with the rice wine to add flavour.

8 Finally, add the sweet and sour sauce, followed by the cornflour dissolved in water; mix thoroughly and serve.

191

Pork chops with Dijon mustard sauce

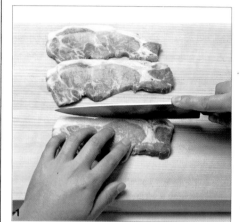

Preparation: 1 hour

12 pork chops
4 tbsp oil
175 g/6 fl oz dry white wine
450 ml/³/₄ pint cream
2 onions
25 g/1 oz butter
4 tbsp gravy made with half
  a stock cube dissolved
  with 15 g/¹/₂ oz butter into
  1¹/₂ tbsp dry white wine
  and 2 tbsp water
3-4 tbsp Dijon mustard
salt and pepper

1 Trim off the fat from the pork chops with a very sharp knife.

2 Melt the butter in a frying pan, add the chopped onions and sauté until a pale golden brown.

3 Heat the oil in another frying pan and when very hot add the lightly floured pork chops. Brown on both sides and then season with a little salt and freshly ground pepper. Pour in the cream and finish cooking the pork chops over a gentle heat; when they are ready remove them from the sauce and keep warm on a heated serving plate.

4 Stir the sautéed onions into the sauce.

5 Stir in the mustard.

6 Add the gravy mixture and reduce over a moderate heat; pour the sauce over the pork, sprinkle with chopped parsley and serve.

Roast pork with prune filling

Preparation: 1 hour
   40 minutes

800 g/1³⁄₄ lb boneless
   shoulder of pork
4 spareribs of pork
1 carrot
1 onion
1 stock cube
6 tbsp oil
175 ml/6 fl oz red wine
1 tbsp pearl barley
15 g/¹⁄₂ oz melted butter
1 tsp soy sauce
1 tbsp plain flour
salt and pepper

For the filling:
20 dried prunes, soaked for
   30 minutes in warm
   water, drained and then
   left to stand for 1 hour in
   red wine.

1   Unroll the shoulder roast and trim.

2   Drain the prunes and reserve the wine. Stone the prunes and arrange 10 of them at one end of the rectangle of pork. Sprinkle with a little salt and freshly ground pepper and roll up the meat so that the prunes end up in the middle. Tie the roll with string.

3   Pour 4 tablespoons of oil into a roasting pan, place the meat in the pan and sprinkle with salt and freshly ground pepper; arrange the spareribs, the coarsely chopped onion and carrot around the rolled pork and brush the meat with the remaining oil. Place in a preheated oven 200°C/400°F/mark 6 and roast for 35 minutes, turning the pork frequently and basting with the juice.

4   When the pork is crisp and well browned, take up and set aside. Place the roasting pan over a low heat and pour in the reserved heated wine into which the stock cube has been crumbled. Stir well.

5   Mix the barley, melted butter, 1 teaspoon soy sauce and 1 tablespoon flour. Add this mixture to the sauce and stir until it thickens.

6   Strain the sauce through a metal sieve into a saucepan.

7   Add the remaining soaked prunes to the sauce, cook for 20 minutes over a gentle heat. When the meat has cooled, remove the string and slice. Arrange in a shallow, ovenproof dish, together with some of the sauce, cover with foil and heat in the oven. Serve with the prunes and garnish with watercress. Serve the remaining sauce in a sauceboat.

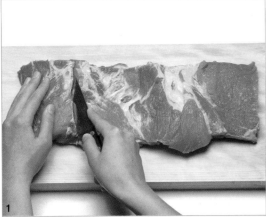

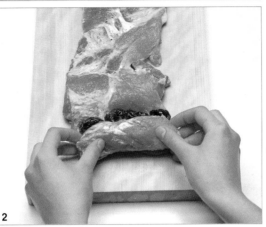

Pork crown roast

Serves 6

Preparation: 2 hours
   30 minutes

9 pork spareribs, uncut

For the stuffing:
125 g/4 oz finely chopped or
   minced cooked ham
125 g/4 oz finely chopped or
   minced pork
80 g/3 oz fresh soft
   breadcrumbs soaked in 6
   tbsp milk and squeezed
   out

2 tbsp freshly grated
Parmesan
1 egg
1 tbsp Dijon mustard
few drops Worcestershire
   sauce
small bunch parsley, finely
   chopped
oil
6 tbsp stock
salt and pepper

1   Trim the ends of the spareribs by cutting away about 4 cm/1¹/₂ in of meat from between the ribs and making small slits between the bones at the meaty end so that the rack can be bent around (smooth, bonier side outward) to form a crown.

2   Tie up the crown roast and place in a roasting pan greased with oil.

3   *To prepare the stuffing:* Mix together the chopped ham, pork, egg, parsley and the grated Parmesan.

4   Add the fresh fine breadcrumbs, the mustard, the Worcestershire sauce, a pinch of salt and a little freshly ground pepper. Mix thoroughly with a wooden spoon until well blended and smooth.

5   Spoon the stuffing into the centre of the crown roast.

6   Cover the crown loosely with foil and cook in a hot oven (200°C/400°F/mark 6) for 1¹/₂ hours. After about 20 minutes pour 6 tablespoons of hot stock into the roasting pan and baste the meat at frequent intervals with the combined juices and stock from the bottom of the pan. When the roast pork is ready to serve, place a small paper crown over each trimmed bone. Garnish with tomatoes and parsley.

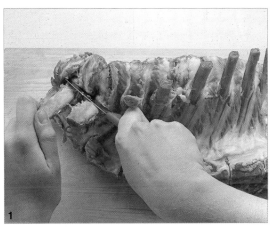

Extra special terrine

Preparation: 1 hour
   50 minutes

275 g/10 oz finely chopped
   or minced pork
225 g/8 oz finely chopped or
   minced beef
125 g/4 oz finely minced
   chicken
225 g/8 oz chicken livers
175 g/6 oz fresh pork fat
pinch of thyme
1 bay leaf

1 tablespoon shelled
   pistachio nuts
2 chicken breasts
2 tbsp brandy
2 tbsp Madeira
2 tbsp sherry
25 g/1 oz butter
salt and pepper

Serve with a little chopped
aspic jelly*, gherkins and hot
French bread.

1 Cut the two chicken breasts into four fillets. Place in a dish with two thirds of the fresh pork fat cut in strips. Pour over the sherry and Madeira and leave for 30 minutes.

2 Melt the butter in a cast-iron frying pan, add half the chicken livers and sauté, seasoning with salt and pepper; sprinkle with the brandy and cook until this has evaporated.

3 Blend the remaining diced pork fat and chicken livers until almost a paste. Transfer to a bowl.

4 Remove the skin from the pistachio nuts by pouring boiling water on them and draining immediately; the skins will then rub off. Chop finely and season.

5 Mix the nuts, chicken liver paste, minced pork, beef and minced chicken into a smooth, even mixture.

6 Butter a rectangular terrine, cover the bottom with a layer of the ground meat and nut mixture; place two chicken fillets flat on top of this, together with a few strips of pork fat. Cover with another layer of mixture. Use a piping bag to layer the meat mixture if you like.

7 Arrange the sautéed chicken livers in a line down the centre.

8 Cover with another layer of meat mixture and continue layering until all the ingredients have been used. Sprinkle with a little thyme, press the bay leaf into the surface and cover the terrine. Place in a roasting pan half-filled with boiling water (lay a tea towel on the bottom of the roasting pan). Cook for about 1 hour at 190°C/375°F/mark 5. Allow to cool completely before cutting into slices.

Chicken Waterzooi

Preparation: 1 hour
20 minutes

1 1.4-kg/3-lb chicken,
jointed
1 large onion
3 celery hearts
3 large leeks (green tops
removed)
1¹/₂ litres/2¹/₂ pints veal stock
(made from raw veal, 1
onion, 2 small carrots, 1
celery stalk, 1 bouquet
garni and 2 peppercorns)

3 egg yolks
1 tbsp finely chopped
parsley
2 tbsp grated Parmesan
15 g/¹/₂ oz unsalted butter
1¹/₂ tsp cornflour
salt

This well-known Belgian
dish is traditionally served
on special occasions. There
is an equally popular version
using fish.

1   Wash the celery hearts and the trimmed white part of the leeks; dry, then slice into thin strips.

2   Butter a deep heavy-bottomed enamel pot; place the celery, leeks and chopped onion in the bottom and then place the chicken pieces on top. Cover the chicken with veal stock.

3   Place a circle of buttered wax paper over the pot and seal firmly with the lid. Bring slowly to the boil, lower the heat and simmer gently for an hour. Remove from the heat, take up the chicken pieces and transfer to a heated dish. Cover and keep warm.

4   Beat the egg yolks with the chopped parsley and add the grated Parmesan cheese. Trickle the hot stock from the pot, reserving the vegetables, in a thin stream onto the beaten egg yolks, whisking vigorously.

5   Mix 1¹/₂ teaspoons of cornflour together with a little water or stock and add to the liquid, stirring well. Return this mixture to the heat and simmer gently, stirring constantly, for about 10 minutes or until the sauce has become creamy and thick.

6   Pour the sauce over the chicken pieces and vegetables, arranged in a dish, and serve immediately.

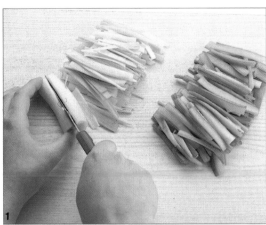

New Castile chicken with apples

Preparation: 1 hour
45 minutes

1 1.6-1.8-kg/3½-4-lb
chicken
2 apples
juice of 1 lemon
2 tbsp brandy
125 g/4 oz sliced bacon or
salt pork
175 ml/6 fl oz dry white wine
4 tbsp oil
few coarsely ground
peppercorns
salt and pepper

202

1   Wash and dry the chicken and season the cavity with a pinch of salt, the coarsely ground peppercorns and the lemon juice.

2   Wash, peel and core the apples, dip in acidulated water if wished to prevent them from discolouring, and cut one in half. Push one half well down into the chicken's cavity, followed by the whole apple and then by the remaining half.

3   Sew up the opening or secure with a skewer; sprinkle the chicken with a little salt and pepper and wrap the slices of bacon or salt pork around it, securing with small skewers.

4   Place the chicken in a casserole dish with the oil and cook in a hot oven at 200°C/400°F/mark 6, turning once or twice so that it browns evenly; after 30 minutes mix the brandy with the wine and pour over the chicken.

5   Continue cooking for another 40-50 minutes or until the meat is tender and the juices run clear when the thigh is pierced with a knife. Baste frequently with the cooking juices and oil.

6   When the chicken is cooked, joint into four pieces and serve at once, garnishing each serving with half an apple.

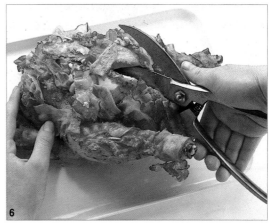

Tunisian chicken

Preparation: 1 hour
   30 minutes

1 1.6-1.8-kg/3¹/₂-4-lb
   chicken
8 tbsp oil
125 g/4 oz stoned green
   olives
1 tsp anchovy paste (made
   by crushing 1-2 anchovy
   fillets into a smooth paste)
275 g/10 oz tinned tomatoes
1 clove garlic
pepper

1   Wash and dry the chicken and joint into serving pieces.

2   Heat the oil in a large heavy-bottomed saucepan and brown the chicken pieces all over, turning frequently so that they cook evenly. Season with a little freshly ground pepper. When the chicken is browned, take out the pieces and keep warm.

3   Place the tomatoes in a large, deep frying pan, crushing them with a fork to break them up. Stir in the anchovy paste and a couple of spoonfuls of water and simmer for a few minutes.

4   Add the whole peeled garlic clove, then the chicken pieces followed by the olives.

5   Simmer over a low heat for 30-40 minutes, stirring now and then, and add a few spoonfuls of hot water if the sauce reduces too rapidly.

6   Remove and discard the garlic; place the chicken portions on a heated serving platter and cover with the sauce. Serve at once.

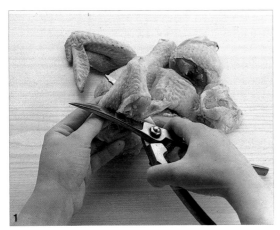

Spicy tomato chicken

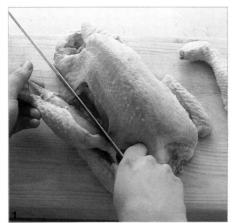  

Preparation: 1 hour
30 minutes

1 1.6-1.8-kg/3$^{1}/_{2}$-4-lb
chicken
4 large onions
2 large crisp apples
125 g/4 oz butter
1 tbsp tomato purée
3 tbsp coconut milk
175 ml/6 fl oz double cream
2 tbsp lemon juice
pinch of powdered bay leaf
pinch of thyme
pinch of cinnamon
$^{1}/_{2}$ litre/1 pint chicken stock
salt and pepper
$^{1}/_{2}$ tbsp garam masala

1 Wash the chicken, dry
and cut into serving pieces.

2 Melt the butter in a large,
heavy-bottomed saucepan
over a moderate heat; add
the sliced onions, the apples,
peeled, cored and chopped,
and the cinnamon. Fry
gently for 5 minutes.

3 Add the chicken portions
and brown for 5 minutes,
stirring and turning
frequently.

4 Add the chicken stock, a
pinch of salt, a little freshly
ground pepper, the thyme
and powdered bay leaf and
simmer gently for 30
minutes.

5 Sprinkle in the garam
masala and add the tomato
purée mixed with the
coconut milk. Continue
cooking over a low heat for
8-10 minutes, until the
sauce has reduced and
thickened slightly.

6 Just before serving, stir
in the cream, mixed with the
lemon juice. Reheat gently
and serve with basmati rice.

Chinese fried chicken

Preparation: 40 minutes

2 spring chicken leg quarters
$^1/_2$ beaten egg
25 g/1 oz cornflour
few drops sesame oil
    (optional)
oil for frying

To flavour:
$^1/_4$ tsp salt
2-3 drops soy sauce
1 tsp rice wine or dry sherry
pinch of pepper

1   Wash and trim the chicken legs; dry with kitchen towel. Using a cleaver, chop through the bone into triangular, bite-size pieces.

2   Mix the beaten egg and the flavouring ingredients together in a bowl and add the chicken pieces.

3   Sprinkle with the cornflour and mix well. Leave to stand for 5 minutes. If a slightly stronger flavour is preferred, add a few drops sesame oil.

4   Heat plenty of oil in a wok, or deep-fryer, to 180°C/350°F/mark 4.

5   Lower the chicken pieces into the hot oil one by one, working as quickly as possible to ensure even cooking.

6   Adding the chicken to the oil will have lowered the temperature to about 150°C/300°F/mark 2. Maintain this lower temperature by turning down the heat; when the chicken is half done, remove the pieces from the oil and prick them with a skewer to make them cook through more quickly. Lower them into the oil once more.

7   When the chicken is nearly cooked, increase the heat so that the oil is really hot; this will make it easier to drain the chicken so that it does not taste oily.

8   If desired, the flavour can be heightened by stir-frying the drained chicken pieces briefly in another frying pan with a few drops of sesame oil and a tablespoon of finely chopped leek.

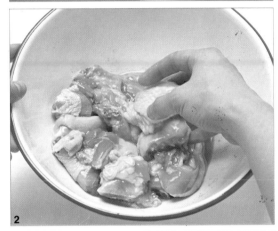

Curried chicken casserole

Preparation: 1 hour
   10 minutes

4 chicken breasts
4 large mushrooms
1 onion
1 clove garlic
1 egg yolk
225 ml/8 fl oz dry white wine
25 g/1 oz butter
2 peeled, boiled potatoes
600 ml/1 pint milk
50 g/2 oz flour
2 tbsp grated Parmesan
1 tbsp mild curry powder
salt and pepper

1   Peel and slice the onion, dice the chicken breasts; wash, dry and slice the mushrooms.

2   Melt the butter in a deep frying pan and gently fry the diced chicken, onion and finely chopped garlic.

3   Pour in the wine and continue cooking until it has evaporated. Season with salt and freshly ground pepper and then take up the chicken, mushrooms and onion with a slotted spoon, and keep warm. Leave the cooking juices in the frying pan.

4   Stir the flour into the juices and fat and add the curry powder.

5   Heat the milk to just below boiling point and gradually add to the curry mixture, stirring constantly.

6   Simmer for 5-10 minutes, whisking until the sauce is smooth and creamy.

7   Meanwhile, boil the potatoes and mash into a bowl. Stir in the egg yolk and season with salt and freshly ground pepper, mixing very thoroughly.

8   Butter a deep casserole dish and cover the bottom with one third of the chicken mixture; cover with half the sauce and sprinkle with half the grated Parmesan cheese. Arrange the rest of the chicken mixture on top and cover with the remaining sauce and cheese. Put a fluted nozzle on a piping bag and spoon the mashed potatoes into the bag; pipe a decorative border around the edge of the dish. Place under a hot grill until the top is a pale golden brown. Serve straight from the casserole dish while very hot.

Peking duck

Preparation: 5 hours
    30 minutes

1 whole duck, weighing
    about 3 kg/6¹/₂ lb, plucked
    but undrawn and with the
    head left on
about 5 cm/2 in of the white
    parts of 12 spring onions
2 tbsp molasses or treacle
24 pancakes*, 10 cm/4 in in
    diameter

For the sauce:
3 tbsp sugar
3 tbsp sweet bean paste
2 tbsp sesame oil
(This sauce can be replaced
by hoisin sauce, which is
readily available from
Oriental stores)

1   Wash the duck and cut
off the feet. Make sharp
notches all round the end of
the spring onions along the
grain of the stem. Place in a
bowl of iced water for 1 to 2
hours so that the ends curl
into feathery flowers.

2   With a small, sharp knife
pierce the duck's neck in the
front below the head,
making a cut down large
enough to insert a straw
between the skin and the
flesh; blow air between the
skin and flesh until the
whole duck is expanded;
this is vital to achieve crackly
yet succulent skin.

3   Make a small slit, and
draw the duck.

4   Wash the duck inside and out and sew the slit up tightly with kitchen thread or cotton.

5   Trim off the wing tips and hang the duck up over a basin.

6   Pour about 1 litre/1¹/₂ pints boiling water over the duck; leave it to dry a little. Combine the molasses with 225 ml/8 fl oz boiling water and pour evenly all over the bird; baste well and repeat the process several times. Leave the bird hung up in a warm dry place or in the sun for up to 4 hours or until the skin is completely dry. Cut the head off the duck and place, breast downward, in a large roasting pan and roast in a preheated oven at 200°C/400°F/mark 6 for 20 minutes. Turn and continue cooking for a further 20 minutes. Place the roasting pan in a pan of hot water over a low heat for a few minutes; then return to the oven for a final 20 minutes' roasting, turning again half-way through.

7   Prepare the sauce: mix the sugar with the sweet bean paste and 6 tablespoons of water. Heat a wok and pour in the sesame oil, add the sauce mixture and cook until it thickens. As an alternative, ready-made hoisin sauce does very well.

8   Carve meat into thin slices. Each person places some meat in a pancake, brushes sauce over it using the spring onions, and rolls up the pancake.

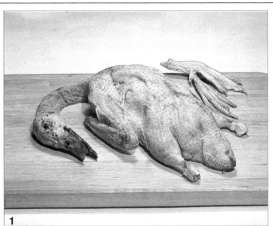

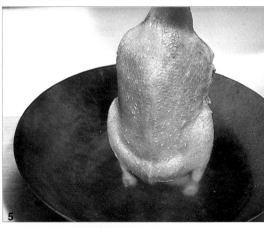

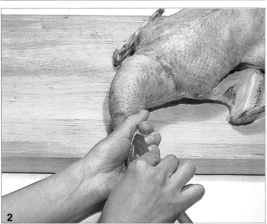

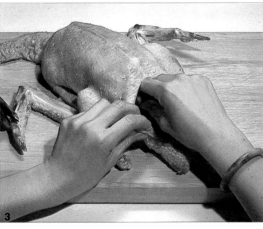

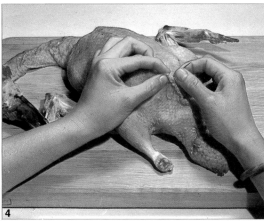

Duck à l'orange

Preparation: 2 hours

1 1.8-kg/4-lb duck
125 g/4 oz butter
2 oranges
peel of 1 orange
225 ml/8 fl oz light stock
1¹/₂ tbsp potato flour or
 cornflour
175 ml/6 fl oz dry sherry
2 tbsp Curaçao
salt and pepper

This simplified version of the
classic French dish makes a
spectacular main course for
a special dinner party.
Garnish with triangles of
bread fried in butter
arranged around the edge of
the serving dish.

214

1   Wash the duck and dry well. Place a small piece of butter inside the cavity and rub a little butter over the less fatty parts of the breast; season inside and out with salt and freshly ground pepper. Pierce skin all over with a fork.

2   Place the duck on a rack in a large roasting pan in an oven preheated to 220°C/425°F/mark 7, turning the heat down to 180°C/350°F/mark 4 after 15 minutes. A 1.8-kg/4-lb duck will take about 1½ hours total cooking time. Alternatively, cook over direct heat in a large deep saucepan. Pierce the breast with the prongs of a fork; when they slide in easily, remove the duck from the roasting pan and keep warm. Reserve the cooking juices.

3   *To prepare the orange sauce:* Pare off the rind of an orange, leaving behind the pith. Blanch in boiling water for a few minutes.

4   Drain off the water, dry the rind and cut into very thin strips; place in a bowl with the Curaçao. Pour the boiling stock into the juices in the roasting pan. Stir in the potato flour or cornflour mixed with the sherry and cook over a high heat until the liquid has reduced by about one third.

5   Add the orange peel and Curaçao and leave to simmer, stirring occasionally for about 5-10 minutes. Remove from heat.

6   Peel the other oranges, removing all the pith, membrane and seeds from each segment.

7   Cut the duck into pieces and arrange on a heated serving platter; pour over the orange sauce and decorate with the orange segments.

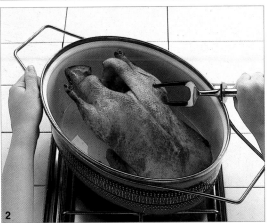

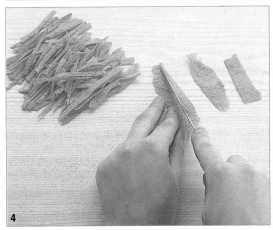

Spanish almond duck

Preparation: 2 hours

1 1.8-kg/4-lb duck, liver
   reserved
flour
125 g/4 oz fresh pork fat or
   lard
2 shallots
275 g/10 oz tinned tomatoes
24 almonds
1 clove garlic
small bunch parsley
225 ml/8 fl oz dry white wine
salt and pepper

1   Wash the duck, dry thoroughly and joint into serving pieces. Reserve the liver as it is an essential part of this recipe.

2   Melt the finely chopped pork fat in a large, heavy-bottomed saucepan and when it is hot sauté the finely chopped duck's liver for 2 or 3 minutes. Remove with a slotted spoon and keep warm.

3   Sauté the finely sliced shallots until a very pale golden brown, remove these with a slotted spoon and keep warm with the liver.

4   Coat the duck pieces with flour and brown well in the hot fat; season with salt and freshly ground pepper.

5   Add the roughly chopped tomatoes and simmer for about 1 hour, turning and stirring from time to time.

6   Toast the almonds in the oven until light golden brown, then chop them up with the cooked liver, shallots and garlic; place in a bowl and moisten with white wine.

7   Add this mixture to the simmering duck and tomatoes, stir and continue cooking, covered, for about 40 minutes. Serve the duck in its sauce, sprinkled with finely chopped parsley.

Stuffed roast turkey

Serves 6

Preparation: 2 hours
    30 minutes

1 2.5-3.5-kg/5-8-lb turkey
2 apples
225 g/8 oz ham
small bunch parsley
2 sage leaves
2 shallots
175 g/6 oz white bread,
    crusts removed, soaked in
    milk and squeezed out

1 clove
2 eggs
3 tbsp fine breadcrumbs
50 g/2 oz chicken livers
125 g/4 oz butter
salt and pepper

For your Christmas or celebration turkey, a more elaborate stuffing can be used. Instead of ham, use 225 g/½ lb button mushrooms; leave out the apples, shallots and sage and substitute two onions, a chopped carrot, a clove of garlic and two small, finely chopped celery stalks. The turkey liver can be used instead of the chicken livers; sauté all these ingredients, finely chopped, in butter and when they are just cooked, add 2 tablespoons brandy, allow to evaporate and remove from heat. Mix with the eggs, soaked white bread, chopped parsley and a little salt and pepper and then stuff the turkey as opposite.

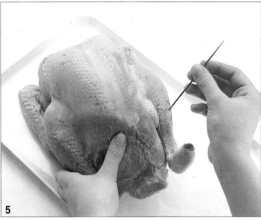

1   Peel, core and chop the apples; sauté them gently in half the butter.

2   Wash and trim the chicken livers; chop finely together with the ham.

3   Transfer to a bowl and add the chopped shallots, sage leaves and parsley. Add the fine breadcrumbs, eggs, the clove, sautéed chopped apple and the white bread moistened with milk; season with salt and a little freshly ground pepper.

4   Mix until the ingredients are well blended. Wash and dry the turkey and season the cavity with salt and pepper; fill with the stuffing.

5   Sew up the opening and place the turkey in a roasting pan. Melt the remaining butter and spread over the breast of the turkey, sprinkle with a little salt and place in the oven, preheated to 200°C/400°F/mark 6.

6   Halfway through the roasting time (allow about 2½-3 hours), cover the turkey with foil and continue roasting, turning the bird from time to time and basting with the juices.

7   When the turkey is cooked (check that the juices run clear when the thigh is pierced) remove from the oven, carve into serving pieces and serve with the stuffing and the juices from the roasting pan.

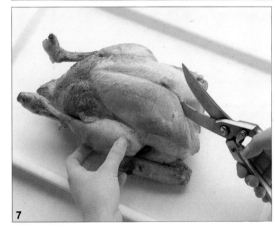

Turkey à la King

Preparation: 1 hour
    25 minutes

800 g/1³/₄ lb turkey breast
  (skin removed)
1 medium onion
125 g/4 oz butter
250 g/9 oz button
  mushrooms
1 celery stalk
2 red peppers
1 bay leaf
1 clove

90 ml/3 fl oz cream
2 egg yolks
225 ml/8 fl oz dry white wine
50 g/2 oz flour
4 tsp coarse salt
2 peppercorns

Serve with rice

1 Slice the onion and place in saucepan with the celery, bay leaf, clove, peppercorns and salt.

2 Place the turkey breast on top of the vegetables and cover with the wine mixed with ½ litre/1 pint of water. Bring to the boil and then simmer very gently for 45 minutes.

3 Allow the turkey breast to cool to room temperature in the cooking liquid; drain, dice and set aside. Discard the celery and bay leaf. Reserve stock and onions.

4 Wash and dry the mushrooms and cut into thin slices; sauté for 15 minutes in 50 g/2 oz butter, stirring frequently, then add to the reserved stock containing the onions.

5 Place the peppers under the grill or hold over a gas burner to scorch the thin outer skin. Peel off the burned skin, remove the stalk, cut open and trim off the pith, removing the seeds. Cut into thin strips and add to the stock.

6 Reserve a little stock to mix with the beaten egg yolks. Melt the remaining butter in a small saucepan, stir in the flour and cook until the *roux* turns a pale golden brown. Add a little of the stock to dilute, then gradually stir into the stock containing the onions, mushrooms and peppers. Cook for 15 minutes, stirring constantly, and then mix in the cream. After a few minutes reduce the heat (or turn off) and trickle in the egg yolks, beaten with a little of the reserved stock.

7 Mix well and stir in the diced turkey. Arrange the rice on a hot serving platter and spoon the turkey and sauce on top.

Roast goose with chestnuts and apples

Serves 4-6

Preparation: 3 hours

1 2-3¹/₂-kg/4¹/₂-8-lb goose
400 g/14 oz peeled
  chestnuts
700 ml/1¹/₄ pints brown
  stock
pinch of chopped tarragon
3 apples
50 g/2 oz sultanas
potato flour or cornflour
4 tbsp oil
salt and pepper

This German recipe includes one of the great variety of stuffings for roast goose from many parts of the world. You can stuff your bird with sausage meat and beans, sauerkraut and apples or vegetables and fruit. Extra cooking time is always allowed for roasting a stuffed bird.

1   Parboil the chestnuts in ¹/₂ litre/1 pint of stock. Wash, quarter and core the apples. Soak the sultanas in warm water.

2   Mix the drained chestnuts with the apple quarters and the well-drained sultanas.

3   Wash, dry and season the goose inside and out with salt, freshly ground pepper and tarragon. Fill the cavity with the fruit and chestnut stuffing.

4   Sew up the opening and place the goose in a roasting pan that has been greased with a tablespoon of oil.

5   Place in a hot oven, preheated to 200°C/400°F/mark 6, and roast for about 2¹/₂-3 hours. Baste from time to time with a little of the remaining hot stock and turn the bird at intervals.

6   When the goose is cooked, transfer it from the roasting pan onto a heated serving platter. Strain the cooking juices and liquid from the pan into a small saucepan; mix the potato flour or cornflour with a little cold water, add to the saucepan and cook for about 5 minutes, stirring constantly. Pour over the goose.

Oriental Spring chicken

Preparation: 1 hour
   10 minutes

2 spring chickens or	3 sage leaves, chopped
poussins, cleaned	1 tbsp tomato purée
1 tin dried chestnuts	4 tbsp stock
50 g/2 oz butter	4 tbsp grated Parmesan
175 ml/6 fl oz dry white wine	1 bay leaf
125 ml/4 fl oz cream	175 ml/6 fl oz Marsala
600 g/1¼ lb bacon or salted	¼ stock cube
smoked belly of pork	1 heaped tsp cornflour
1 small onion	200 ml/7 fl oz oil
80 g/3 oz fine fresh	nutmeg
breadcrumbs	salt and pepper
juice of ½ lemon	

1   Simmer the dried chestnuts for a few minutes then set aside.

2   Chop the onion finely with the bacon and fry in 25 g/1 oz butter with the bay leaf.

3   Add the breadcrumbs, grated Parmesan and lemon juice and mix well.

4   Stir in 1 teaspoon tomato purée followed by about two thirds of the drained chestnuts. Crush them into the mixture with a fork. Season with salt, grated nutmeg, pepper and the sage leaves.

5   Cut the chickens in half and pound flat with the meat mallet. Heat the oil in a very large frying pan and fry each halved chicken over a high heat for 15 minutes, turning frequently. Season, and moisten with a little white wine.

6   Place each halved chicken on a chopping board and cover with a few spoonfuls of the chestnut, cheese and breadcrumb mixture; press one or two of the reserved chestnuts on top. Sprinkle with a little grated Parmesan. Place in the oven (preheated to 180°C/350°F/mark 4) and cook for 10-15 minutes or until golden brown.

7   Make the sauce. Work the cornflour into the remaining softened butter and stir into the cooking juices in the pan. Stir in the remaining tomato paste mixed with the stock and cook over a low heat; when the sauce has thickened slightly, add the Marsala and cream. Crumble the extra stock cube into the sauce and mix well; simmer, stirring constantly, for about 10 minutes. Serve at once, spooning a little sauce on to each plate and placing half a chicken on top. Serve any remaining sauce separately.

Pheasant à la georgienne

Preparation: 1 hour
    30 minutes

1 plump young hen
    pheasant
12 strips bacon or salt pork
20 walnuts
800 g/1³/₄ lb white grapes
175 ml/6 fl oz strained China
    tea
juice of 2 large oranges
175 ml/6 fl oz Marsala
40 g/1¹/₂ oz butter
salt and pepper

1   Wash and dry the pheasant; season the cavity with a little salt and freshly ground pepper.

2   Wrap the fat around the pheasant and secure with wooden skewers.

3   Place in a heavy-bottomed saucepan with the butter, adding the orange juice and the chopped or coarsely broken up walnuts.

4   Place the grapes in a sieve and crush with a wooden spoon, collecting the juice in a bowl. Add to the saucepan together with the Marsala followed by the China tea; cover and simmer for 40 minutes over a gentle heat.

5   When cooked, take up the pheasant, remove the fat and return to the saucepan to brown. Season with a little more salt and freshly ground pepper.

6   When the pheasant has browned, transfer to a heated serving dish and cover with the sauce.

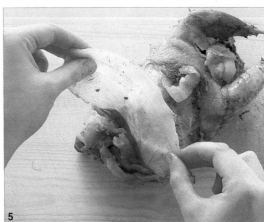

Spanish roast lamb

Preparation: 1 hour
30 minutes

1 1.5-kg/3-3¹/₄-lb shoulder
of baby or milk-fed lamb
4 cloves garlic
125 g/4 oz melted fresh pork
fat
450 g/1 lb new potatoes
several sprigs of rosemary
salt and pepper

This delicious way of
presenting lamb, typical of
traditional Spanish
provincial cooking, is both
simple to prepare and very
nourishing. If young lamb is
difficult to find, use leg from
the youngest, tenderest
lamb available.

1   Peel and crush 3 cloves of garlic and rub into the surface of the lamb or insert into slits in the meat so that it is well flavoured.

2   Sprinkle salt and freshly ground pepper on each side of the shoulder before putting it onto a rotisserie spit. Roast in a preheated oven for 40 minutes or until tender at 220°C/425°F/mark 7; place a roasting pan under the lamb to catch the juices and fat as it cooks.

3   At frequent intervals dip a glazing brush into the fat that collects in the roasting pan and baste the shoulder. Once the lamb has started to brown evenly all over, baste every 5-10 minutes, dipping the brush into the melted fresh pork fat. When the lamb is cooked (a rosy pink inside unless you prefer it well done), remove carefully from spit and wrap in foil to keep warm. Turn oven heat down to 180°C/350°F/ mark 4.

4   Scrub off the skin of the new potatoes and toss in a large bowl with the chopped rosemary, a crushed clove of garlic and coarse salt.

5   Place the potatoes and rosemary in the hot fat left in the roasting pan, and roast for 30 minutes with the oven at 180°C/350°F/mark 4. Turn the potatoes at least once during cooking.

6   When the potatoes are golden brown, unwrap the lamb and place in the pan; leave in the oven for a few minutes. Serve the lamb on a very hot platter, garnished with a few sprigs of rosemary.

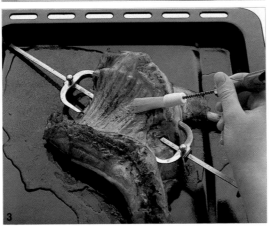

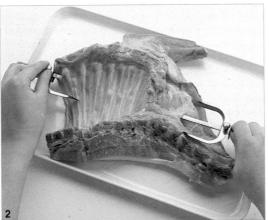

Lamb Provençal

Preparation: 1 hour

700 g/1½ lb boned lamb
   chops
2 courgettes
2 aubergines
2 large but not overripe
   tomatoes
generous pinch mixed dried
   herbs
350 ml/12 fl oz oil
salt and pepper

For the tomato sauce:
12 large ripe tomatoes
½ onion
1 clove garlic
3 tbsp olive oil
salt and pepper

230

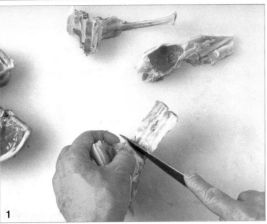

1 If the butcher has not already done so for you, bone the lamb, and slice into thick medallions. Flatten with a meat mallet.

2 Peel lengthwise strips from the courgettes, slice in rounds and fry in half of the oil, preheated until very hot; take up with a slotted spoon and drain on paper towels. Prepare the aubergines in the same way.

3 Heat the remaining oil in the same saucepan and sauté the lamb until well browned on both sides; season with a pinch of salt and freshly ground pepper; take up and set aside on a warm plate.

4 *To prepare the tomato sauce:* Trim, wash and dry the tomatoes; remove the seeds and chop coarsely. Cook slowly in a saucepan with half an onion and a clove of garlic for about 30 minutes. Allow the sauce to reduce and thicken. Pass through a sieve or liquidizer and add a little salt, pepper and olive oil.

5 Grease an oval ovenproof dish with oil and spoon in about 6 tablespoons of the tomato sauce.

6 Arrange the fried vegetables, meat and 2 raw sliced tomatoes in rows across the ovenproof dish, beginning with a row of fried courgettes, then raw tomatoes, followed by fried aubergines and the sautéed lamb. Repeat until all the ingredients have been used up. Sprinkle with the dried herbs.

7 Top with the remaining tomato sauce and bake in a fairly hot oven (180°C/350°F/mark 4) for 20 minutes. Serve immediately.

231

Jellied rabbit mould

Preparation: 1 hour
50 minutes (+ chilling
time)

1 1.5-kg/3-3¹/₂-lb rabbit
900 ml/1¹/₂ pints gelatine
(use 1¹/₂ packets
powdered gelatine
dissolved in 700 ml/1¹/₄
pints light meat stock,
flavoured with
175 ml/6 fl oz sherry,
cooled but still liquid)
175 g/6 oz baby carrots,
sliced into rounds
175 g/6 oz baby onions
125 g/4 oz small mushrooms

175 g/6 oz stoned black olives
175 g/6 oz stoned green
olives
2 tbsp capers
50 g/2 oz butter
225 ml/8 fl oz dry white wine
6 gherkins
2 tbsp oil
2 tbsp wine vinegar
1 clove
1 bay leaf
1 clove garlic
1 tbsp chopped chervil
salt and pepper

1   If the butcher has not already done so for you, joint the rabbit into 7-8 pieces (do not use the head). Brown the rabbit in the butter and oil in a heavy-bottomed saucepan.

2   Season the rabbit pieces with salt and a little freshly ground pepper before adding the onions, sliced mushrooms, clove, bay leaf and garlic.

3   Cook for 15 minutes, then pour in the wine and vinegar. Cover and simmer over a very low heat for 1 hour 20 minutes, turning and mixing occasionally with a wooden spatula.

4   *To prepare the savoury jelly:* While the rabbit and vegetables are cooking, dissolve the gelatine in the hot broth; when it has dissolved stir in the sherry.

5   Rinse out a large mould with cold water and spoon in enough warm gelatine mixture to cover the bottom. Chill in the refrigerator.

6   When this first layer of jelly has set arrange the cooled pieces of rabbit in the mould, layering them with the slices of raw carrot, chervil, sliced mushrooms, onions and the drained, dried capers.

7   Pour a little gelatine into the mould, chill, and proceed with the next layer. When all the rabbit and vegetables have been set in the jelly, finish off with the remaining liquid gelatine and chill for at least 2 hours.

8   To serve the jellied rabbit, dip the mould almost up to its rim in a large bowl of hot water, cover with the serving plate and then turn the mould upside down on the plate. Garnish with gherkins and black and green olives.

Snails à la Bourguignonne

Preparation: About 4 hours

32 large snails, cleaned (or use tinned)
4 carrots
2 medium sized onions
4 shallots
1 clove garlic
1 bouquet garni
coarse salt

For the stuffing:
2 tbsp fine fresh breadcrumbs
275 g/10 oz softened butter
1 tbsp finely chopped shallot mixed with 1 finely chopped clove garlic
2 heaped tbsp finely chopped parsley
pinch mixed spice
salt and pepper

1 If using fresh, cleaned snails, place them in a large saucepan, cover in water and bring slowly to the boil. As they start to come out of the shells, increase the heat and cook for 9 minutes. Remove and rinse under cold running water.

2 Rinse out the cooking pot and place the drained snails in it; cover with fresh water and sprinkle them with coarse sea salt, allowing about 8 g/¹/₄ oz for every 1 litre/1¹/₂ pints of water. Slice the carrots, onions and shallots and add to the salted water, together with the peeled, crushed clove of garlic and the bouquet garni. Bring slowly to the boil and simmer for about 3¹/₂ hours.

3 Drain the snails in a colander. Remove the snails and cut away the hard, black part at each end.

4 Wash the shells in warm water and leave to dry on a cloth laid on a baking tray. Place in a warm oven with the door open.

5 Work the butter with a fork until it is soft and blend in the very finely chopped shallot, the crushed clove of garlic, the finely chopped parsley, a pinch of salt and freshly ground white pepper. Add a pinch of mixed spice and blend well.

6 Place the tinned or prepared snails in their shells and press the butter mixture into the opening of each shell, smoothing it so that it covers the aperture completely. Sprinkle with fine breadcrumbs and a few drops of melted butter. Place in a hot oven (preheated to 230°C/450°F/mark 8) for 8 minutes.

Eggs and Cheese

Eggs in aspic

Preparation: 1 hour

vinegar
salt
4 eggs
powdered aspic for ¹/₂ litre/1
   pint liquid
1¹/₂ tbsp sherry
1 strip red pepper
150 g/5 oz tin prawn or crab
   pâté
225 g/4 oz cooked prawns

1 Bring 1 litre/1³/₄ pints water, 1 teaspoon vinegar and a pinch of salt to the boil in a saucepan. Simmer gently. Poach the eggs in the water for 3 minutes. Remove with a slotted spoon and drain on a tea towel.

2 Prepare the aspic following the manufacturer's instructions and flavour with 1¹/₂ tbsp sherry. Leave to cool.

3 Pour a little aspic into the bottom of four moulds. Place in the freezer to set. Cut the pepper into trefoils and place one on each set layer of aspic. Cover with another layer of aspic and return to the freezer to set.

4 Spoon a little prawn or crab pâté into each mould. Place an egg on top and cover with the remaining aspic. Refrigerate for 2 hours.

5 Dip briefly in hot water to unmould, and garnish with prawns.

Baked eggs with peppers

Preparation: 35 minutes

1 large red pepper
1 large green pepper
2 tbsp oil
1 clove garlic
salt and pepper
1 large onion, chopped
25 g/1 oz butter
4 eggs
tomato ketchup

1   Hold the peppers on a fork over a flame until the skin blisters and can be peeled off. Seed and cut into strips.

2   Place the oil and whole garlic clove in a frying pan and brown. Crush the garlic with a fork, then discard. Add the pepper strips and fry for 2-3 minutes over a high heat; lower the heat and cook for about 10 minutes until tender but still firm. Season.

3   Cook the onion in a small saucepan in 25 g/1 oz butter, adding a few tablespoons of water so that it does not brown.

4   Divide onion between four gratin dishes. Crack an egg into each, season, and cook in a hot oven (220°C/400°F/mark 6) for 5-8 minutes or until set.

5   Remove from the oven, arrange the peppers around the eggs and pour a ring of ketchup around the yolks.

Fried eggs with tomatoes and mushrooms

Preparation: 15 minutes

8 g/¹/₄ oz dried Chinese
    wood-ear mushrooms
2 eggs
pinch of salt
2 ripe tomatoes, skinned
oil for frying
1 tsp sugar
1 tbsp soy sauce

1   Soak the dried
mushrooms in warm water
for 20 minutes, wash well,
dry and chop the larger
pieces in half.

2   Beat the eggs in a bowl
together with a pinch of salt
and chop the tomatoes.

3   Heat a wok and pour in
2 tablespoons oil. When hot,
pour in the eggs.

4   Scoop and turn the
omelette mixture, until just
set. Remove from the wok;
pour in 1¹/₂ tablespoons oil
and heat. Add the chopped
tomato and stir-fry lightly.
When heated through,
return the eggs to the pan,
add the mushrooms and
cook briefly.

5   Sprinkle with the sugar
and soy sauce, and serve.

Tea eggs

Preparation: 1 hour

6 eggs
2 tsp tea leaves
1 star anise
1 tsp sugar
$^1/_4$ tsp salt
1 tbsp soy sauce
2 cucumbers
1 tsp salt
1 tsp hot soybean paste
few drops of sesame oil

1   Hard-boil the 6 eggs and roll against a surface, pressing gently so as to form tiny cracks in the shell.

2   Place in a saucepan of water with the tea, star anise, sugar, salt and soy sauce. Boil gently for up to 1 hour, turning now and then.

3   Remove from the pan and shell carefully, taking care not to tear the delicate skin immediately under the shell.

4   Slice the cucumbers in half vertically, scoring the skin in a trellis pattern, and cut into small pieces. Place in a bowl and sprinkle with 1 teaspon salt; when softened, sprinkle with cold water and drain. In a separate bowl mix the soybean paste, the soy sauce and the sesame oil; add the cucumber and mix.

5   Arrange the cucumber in a bowl and top with the tea eggs.

241

Crêpes with radicchio Treviso style

Preparation: 1 hour

2 eggs
100 g/3⁸¹/₂ oz flour
80 g/3 oz butter
salt
200 ml/7 fl oz milk
2 tbsp oil for frying
450 g/1 lb radicchio
2 shallots
150 ml/5 fl oz white wine
pepper
125 g/4 oz grated Parmesan

For the white sauce:
50 g/2 oz butter
50 g/2 oz flour
1 litre/1³/₄ pints milk

1   Mix together the eggs and the flour in a bowl. Add 25 g/1 oz melted butter and a pinch of salt and gradually stir in the milk.

2   Heat a little oil in a 20-cm/8-in non-stick frying pan. Pour in a little of the crêpe mixture and cook quickly on both sides. Remove and set aside. Repeat until mixture is finished.

3   Slice the radicchio and chop the shallots.

4   Melt 50 g/2 oz butter in a frying pan and fry the radicchio and shallots for about 15 minutes. Add the white wine, season with salt and freshly ground pepper and cook for another 10 minutes.

5   Prepare the white sauce. Melt the butter in a small saucepan, add the flour and stir for 3 minutes. Gradually pour in the hot milk and cook for 10 minutes, stirring constantly. Season with salt and white pepper.

6   Pour half the sauce into the radicchio mixture and spoon a little of this mixture into the centre of each crêpe.

7   Fold each one in four and place in a buttered ovenproof dish.

8   Pour over the remaining white sauce. Sprinkle with Parmesan and bake in a preheated oven at 220°C/425°F/mark 7 for 15 minutes.

Prawn and mushroom crêpes

Preparation: 1 hour

16 crêpes*

For the filling:
225 g/8 oz shelled prawns
1 celery stalk
125 g/4 oz mushrooms
$^1/_2$ onion
1 clove garlic
pinch of grated nutmeg
2 sage leaves
3 tbsp olive oil
fresh breadcrumbs
3 tbsp cream
1 tsp lemon juice
6 tbsp dry vermouth

1 egg yolk
salt and pepper

For the sauce:
40 g/1$^1/_2$ oz butter
40 g/1$^1/_2$ oz flour
$^1/_2$ litre/$^3/_4$ pint light stock
6 tbsp dry white wine
1 egg yolk
1 tbsp tomato purée
salt
white pepper
3 tbsp grated Parmesan
20 g/$^3/_4$ oz butter

1   Prepare the crêpes*. *To prepare the filling:* Chop the onion, garlic clove and celery finely and fry gently in the oil until soft.

2   Add the shelled prawns and sauté for 5 minutes if raw (if cooked, warm through for about a minute); add the washed and chopped mushrooms. Add a little salt and freshly ground pepper, a pinch of grated nutmeg and two chopped sage leaves. Simmer for 10 minutes and then sprinkle in the lemon juice and the breadcrumbs; stir in the vermouth and then the cream and egg yolk.

3   Place equal amounts of this filling on each crêpe and roll up.

4   *To prepare the sauce:* Melt the butter in a saucepan, stir in the flour and gradually add the hot stock, stirring constantly to prevent any lumps forming. Gradually add the dry white wine and season with salt and white pepper. Remove from the heat and whisk in the beaten egg yolk in a thin stream. Stir in the tomato purée.

5   Place the rolled up crêpes in a shallow ovenproof dish and coat evenly with the sauce.

6   Sprinkle with 3 tablespoons grated Parmesan cheese and dot with butter. Place in a preheated oven at 180°C/350°F/mark 4 for 25 minutes until the top is lightly browned.

Crêpes with ricotta and spinach

Preparation: 2 hours

12 crêpes*
350 g/12 oz ricotta cheese
250 g/9 oz cooked chopped
  spinach
2 tbsp grated Parmesan
salt
pepper
nutmeg
few tbsp freshly made
  tomato sauce*
few fresh basil leaves

1   Mix together the crumbled ricotta, spinach, and Parmesan. Season with salt, pepper, and nutmeg.

2   Fill the crêpes with the mixture, roll up and place in a buttered ovenproof dish.

3   Cook at 190°C/375°F/ mark 5 for 10 minutes. Serve with tomato sauce and garnish with basil.

Crêpe tower

Preparation:
  1 hour 20 minutes

9 crêpes*
salt
55 g/2 oz butter
15 g/¹⁄₂ oz flour
300 ml/¹⁄₂ pint milk
250 g/9 oz frozen chopped
  spinach
2 cloves garlic
few fresh basil leaves
1 sprig parsley
225 g/8 oz puréed tomatoes
175 g/6 oz black olives
1 onion

1   Place 15 g/¹⁄₂ oz butter in a saucepan and add one whole clove garlic. Add the spinach and a pinch of salt and cook gently for about 15 minutes until the liquid has evaporated. Discard the garlic.

2   Chop together one clove of garlic, the basil and parsley. Cook briefly in 15 g/¹⁄₂ oz butter, then add the tomatoes. Season, then simmer for 15 minutes until thickened.

3   Stone and chop the olives, reserving three whole ones; chop the onion and fry in 25 g/1 oz butter; add 15 g/¹⁄₂ oz flour, then gradually stir in the milk. Season and cook for 10 minutes, stirring occasionally.

4   Line a soufflé dish with foil and place a crêpe in the bottom. Cover with half the spinach, then layer the crêpes alternately with the tomato sauce, chopped olives and white sauce, ending with a crêpe. Refrigerate for 2 hours.

5   Unmould and garnish with the reserved olives and a few onion rings.

Savoury filled omelette

Preparation: 1 hour
    15 minutes

2 potatoes
125 g/4 oz sliced bacon
1 red onion
1¹/₂ tbsp oil
6 eggs
1 tbsp grated cheese
salt
pepper
15 g/¹/₂ oz butter

1   Peel and dice the potatoes. Cut the bacon into thin strips. Peel and finely chop the onion.

2   Fry the bacon and onion for a few minutes in 1¹/₂ tbsp oil in a non-stick frying pan, then add the potatoes.

3   Season. Cover and cook for 20 minutes, stirring occasionally.

4   Beat the eggs in a bowl and stir in the grated cheese. Season.

5   Melt the butter in a large frying pan. Pour the eggs in, and tilt to spread evenly over the bottom. Cook over a fairly high heat.

6   Lower the heat and place the potatoes, onion and bacon in the middle. Fold in half, and cook for a few more seconds.

Five-colour omelette

Preparation: 20 minutes

2 slices cooked ham
$^1/_2$ bunch spring onions
100 g/3-4 oz boiled fresh or
     tinned bamboo shoots
3 Chinese mushrooms
6 eggs
$^1/_2$ tsp salt
$^1/_2$ tsp sugar
oil for frying

1   Cut the ham into thin strips; chop the spring onions.

2   Shred the bamboo shoots and chop finely. Clean and slice the mushrooms.

3   Beat the eggs in a bowl. (Always use very fresh eggs when making an omelette.)

4   Mix in the salt and sugar and beat the eggs briefly but energetically, lifting the mixture to incorporate as much air as possible.

5   Add the ham, spring onions, bamboo shoots and mushrooms and stir well.

6   Heat 2 tablespoons oil in a wok; pour the whole omelette mixture into the wok at once, cook until just set, using a spatula or a Chinese scoop or turner to make sure the ingredients are evenly spread throughout the omelette.

7   When the omelette has set on one side, turn it over, dividing it into three portions; then scoop the three portions together again.

8   When the omelette has set into a nicely rounded shape, cover and cook for a very short time, and then serve. The whole of this operation will only take a few minutes.

Chinese eggs with pork

400 g/14 oz pork belly
4 Chinese mushrooms
1 leek
50 g/2 oz dried prawns
2-3 tbsp peanut oil
5 tbsp soy sauce
1 tbsp rice wine
1 tsp sugar
pinch Chinese five-spice
  powder
4 eggs

1   Dice the pork belly into
1-cm/$^{1}/_{2}$-in cubes.

2   Chop the mushrooms
and leek. Soak the prawns
in water and, when plump,
drain, reserving the liquid.

3   Heat the oil in a wok and
stir-fry the leek and prawns.

4   Add the mushrooms and
pork belly and stir-fry; add
the soy sauce, rice wine,
sugar and five-spice powder.
Transfer to a deep
saucepan.

5   Add enough stock made
up from the prawn liquid,
topping up with water if
necessary, to cover all the
ingredients.

6   Add the eggs, peeled
and hard-boiled. Cover and
cook for about 1 hour.

Cheese ring with herbs

Serves 6

Preparation: 45 minutes

150 g/5 oz full fat cream
  cheese with herbs
4 soft processed cheese
  portions (125 g/4 oz)
250 g/9 oz cream cheese
3 tbsp vodka
salt and pepper
1 sprig parsley
15 g/¹/₂ oz butter
few radishes
chives

1   Mash the herb cream
cheese in a bowl until
creamy. Add the processed
cheese portions and mix
well.

2   Add the plain cream
cheese, continuing to beat,
and gradually stir in the
vodka. When smooth and
well blended season with
salt and pepper.

3   Finely chop the parsley.
Add to the mixture and stir
well.

4   Lightly butter a ring
mould and pour in the
mixture, pressing firmly with
the back of a wooden
spoon. Refrigerate for 2
hours.

5   Dip the mould into hot
water for a few seconds,
then turn out onto a serving
dish. Decorate with radishes,
parsley and chives.

Soft cheese bites

Serves 6

Preparation: 15 minutes

400 g/14 oz goat's cheese
12 slices bread
2 eggs
oil
salt
4 tbsp dried breadcrumbs
3 tbsp grated Parmesan

1   Shape the goat's cheese into equal rounds. From each slice of bread cut two circles slightly bigger than the cheese rings.

2   Beat the eggs with 1 tbsp oil and a pinch of salt; in a separate dish mix the dried breadcrumbs and grated cheese.

3   Dip the cheese rings and bread circles first in beaten egg and then in the breadcrumb mixture. Place a cheese ring on each circle of bread.

4   Place the cheese bites in a heatproof pan and brown under a hot grill for 5 minutes.

Cheese soufflé

Preparation: 1 hour

50 g/2 oz butter
grated Parmesan
40 g/1½ oz plain flour
400 ml/14 fl oz milk
salt
nutmeg
80 g/3 oz Emmental, grated
4 eggs, separated

1   Butter a 20-cm/8-in soufflé dish and sprinkle the inside with grated Parmesan.

2   Melt the butter in a saucepan, then stir in the sifted flour, mixing well to avoid lumps. Cook for 2-3 minutes, then gradually stir in the hot milk. Cook over a low heat for 10 minutes.

3   Season with salt and grated nutmeg, then add the Emmental.

4   Cool slightly, then stir in the egg yolks one at a time, mixing in thoroughly.

5   Whisk the egg whites with a pinch of salt until stiff, then gently fold into the sauce using a metal spoon.

6   Pour the mixture into the soufflé dish (it should fill no more than three quarters of the dish). Cook in a preheated oven at 200°C/400°F/mark 6 for about 30 minutes without opening the oven door. Serve at once before the soufflé collapses.

Fried cheese

Preparation: 50 minutes

275 g/10 oz Emmental
225 g/8 oz puréed tomatoes
2 cloves garlic
oil for frying
salt
oregano
200 g/7 oz plain flour
200 ml/7 fl oz milk
2 eggs, separated

1   Cut the Emmental into wide strips.

2   Prepare the sauce: heat the puréed tomatoes together with the peeled garlic in 3 tbsp oil. Add salt to taste and cook over a high heat for 10-15 minutes, adding a generous pinch of oregano.

3   Place the flour in a bowl and gradually work in the milk, beating with a whisk. Add 1$^{1}/_{2}$ tbsp oil, then stir in the yolks one at a time. Whisk the egg whites until stiff, then, using a metal spoon, fold carefully into the batter.

4   Heat a generous quantity of oil in a frying pan. Dip the cheese strips in the batter, using a fork, then deep fry until golden in the oil, which should not be too hot (the batter should not swell up). Drain the cheese strips on kitchen paper and serve hot with the sauce.

Ham and cheese pudding

Preparation: 1 hour
   30 minutes

25 g/1 oz butter
4 tbsp grated Parmesan
16 slices bread
350 ml/12 fl oz milk
225 g/8 oz cooked ham,
   sliced
225 g/8 oz mozzarella, thinly
   sliced
salt
6 eggs

1   Butter a high-sided soufflé dish and sprinkle with 2 tbsp Parmesan.

2   Cut the crusts off the bread and briefly dip four, one at a time, in the milk; place them in the soufflé dish to form the bottom layer.

3   Place a layer of ham strips on top; add a few mozzarella slices and a pinch of salt. Repeat the layers, ending with a layer of bread.

4   Beat together the eggs, 3-4 tbsp milk, 2 tbsp Parmesan and a pinch of salt until frothy, then pour into the soufflé dish; pierce the surface with a cocktail stick so that the beaten egg can penetrate to the bottom layers. Leave to stand for 10 minutes.

5   Place a few pieces of butter on the top, then transfer to a preheated oven (180°C/350°F/mark 4) for about 1 hour until golden brown and well risen. Unmould to serve.

Orange or sultana crêpes

For the batter:
150 ml/5 fl oz milk
120 ml/4 fl oz single cream
4 tbsp orange liqueur
50 g/2 oz plain flour
50 g/2 oz sugar
¹/₄ tsp salt
3 egg yolks
1 egg white
40 g/1¹/₂ oz butter

Orange filling:
50 g/2 oz butter
125 g/4 oz sugar
1 tsp grated orange peel
1 tbsp brandy
8 tbsp orange juice
orange slices

Sultana filling:
125 g/4 oz sultanas
3 tbsp rum
50 g/2 oz butter
125 g/4 oz sugar

1 Pour the milk, cream and orange liqueur into a mixing bowl; sift the flour, sugar and salt into the liquid and mix well – there should be no lumps.

2 Beat the egg yolks and white separately and fold into the mixture.

3 Cover and leave for 1 hour.

4 Melt the butter and add to the mixture.

5 Over a moderate heat warm a frying pan (at least 18 cm/7 in wide) which has been greased with a film of butter or lard. When the frying pan starts to smoke, pour in just enough batter to cover the base. Shake to prevent the crêpe from sticking.

6 When the first side is golden, turn the crêpe over to cook the other side. Repeat the operation until all the batter is used.

7 *For orange crêpes:* Beat together the butter, sugar, grated rind and liqueur. Add the orange juice. Cook over a low heat until the mixture thickens. Spread each crêpe with a spoonful of the sauce, roll and arrange on a serving dish. Pour the remaining sauce over the crêpe and decorate with slices of orange.

8 *For sultana crêpes:* First soak the sultanas in the rum and melt the butter and sugar together in a saucepan. Add the sultanas and spirit. When the sauce thickens, remove from the heat. Spread a spoonful of this sauce on each crêpe, roll and arrange on a serving dish; pour the remaining sauce over the crêpes and serve.

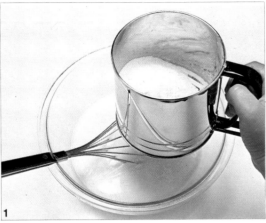

Vanilla bavarian cream

2 (8 g/¼ oz) envelopes
   unflavoured gelatine
½ litre/1 pint milk
250 g/9 oz sugar
6 egg yolks
1 tsp cornflour
1 tbsp vanilla sugar
400 ml/14 fl oz double
   cream
almond or sunflower oil

1   Sprinkle the gelatine into a little hot water in a cup to dissolve it.

2   Reserve a small glass of milk; put the rest of the milk and sugar in a saucepan over a low heat.

3   With a balloon whisk, beat the egg yolks, cornflour and vanilla sugar. Add the reserved cold milk. When the milk in the saucepan comes to the boil add it to the egg mixture.

4   Return the mixture to the heat; when it is almost at boiling point, remove and stir in the gelatine. Do not allow to boil.

5   Leave to cool, stirring occasionally.

6   Whip the cream and fold gently into the mixture. Turn into a mould which has been brushed with almond or sunflower oil. Refrigerate for at least 5 hours before serving.

Crème caramel

175 g/6 oz sugar
7 egg yolks
3 egg whites
few drops vanilla essence
¹/₂ litre/1 pint milk

1   To make the caramel, heat 50 g/2 oz sugar in a saucepan with a few teaspoons of water, stirring until the syrup turns light brown. Remove from the heat and use immediately.

2   Pour equal quantities of caramel into small moulds.

3   Beat the egg yolks and remaining sugar together in a large bowl until thick and creamy.

4   Whisk the egg whites until very stiff and fold into the egg and sugar mixture.

5   Add the vanilla essence to the milk and bring to the boil. Allow to cool a little, then pour into the egg mixture and mix well.

6   Place the moulds in a baking tin and fill with water to come half-way up the sides of the moulds.

7   Divide the custard between the moulds, pouring it through a sieve first to eliminate any lumps.

8   Place the tin in a preheated oven at 170°C/325°F/mark 3 for 20-30 minutes or until the custards are firm. Stand them in a cool place for several hours or overnight.

263

Baked cheesecake

For the pastry:
125 g/4 oz plain flour
125 g/4 oz sugar
$^{1}/_{2}$ tsp salt
125 g/4 oz butter
1 egg

For the filling:
275 g/10 oz cream cheese
2 eggs
40 g/1$^{1}/_{2}$ oz melted butter
25 g/1 oz plain flour
50 g/2 oz sugar
$^{1}/_{2}$ tsp vanilla essence
$^{1}/_{2}$ tsp salt
90 ml/3 fl oz whipping cream
2 tbsp sugar

For the glaze:
1 egg yolk
2 tbsp icing sugar
1 tbsp water

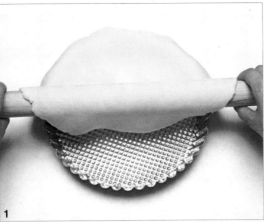

1   Preheat oven to 200°C/400°F/mark 6. In a medium bowl, combine flour and salt. Cut in butter until pieces are size of small peas. Add 3 tablespoons water; toss with fork until all flour is moistened and mixture begins to form a ball. Add more water to crumbs in bottom of bowl, if necessary. Gather dough into a flat ball. Roll out to a 30-cm/12-in circle.

2   Fit pastry into a 25-cm/10-in fluted tin, pressing to side and bottom of tin. Do not stretch.

3   Prick lightly with a fork.

4   In a large bowl, beat together cream cheese, eggs and butter.

5   Sift flour gradually into cheese mixture. Blend well. Add vanilla and orange peel.

6   In a separate bowl, whip the cream, gradually adding the sugar.

7   Fold whipped cream carefully into the cheese mixture.

8   Pour cheese mixture into pastry-lined tin; smooth top. To make glaze, combine egg yolk, sugar and water. Glaze top of cheesecake lightly. Bake 20 minutes or until golden brown. Makes 1 (25-cm/10-in) cheesecake.

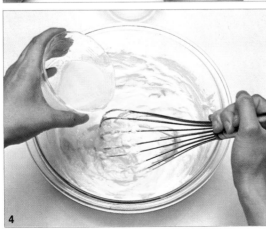

Vegetables

Ravioli filled with mushrooms

Preparation: 1¹/₂ hours

500 g/1-1¹/₄ lb ravioli
salt
50 g/2 oz butter
4 leaves fresh sage
2-3 sprigs fresh thyme
175 g/6 oz grated Parmesan

For the pasta:
250 g/9 oz flour
3 eggs, salt

For the filling:
225 g/8 oz mushrooms
40 g/1¹/₂ oz butter
1 clove garlic
salt
175 g/6 oz ricotta
1 tsp chopped fresh parsley
2 tbsp grated Parmesan
black pepper
1 egg white

1   Rinse, dry and cut the mushrooms into strips.

2   Melt 40 g/1½ oz butter in a frying pan. Add the mushrooms, minced garlic and a pinch of salt and cook until the mushrooms are tender.

3   Mix together in a bowl the ricotta, mushrooms, chopped parsley and Parmesan. Sprinkle with freshly ground black pepper and stir well.

4   Prepare the pasta* and cut into 5-cm/2-in squares using a pastry wheel.

5   Roll the filling into little balls and place one in the centre of each square of pasta. Brush the edges with water or egg white and fold over to form a triangle. Press the edges firmly together.

6   Put into boiling salted water and cook for 5 minutes or until *al dente*. Drain and serve in heated dishes.

7   Meanwhile, melt 50 g/2 oz butter in a small frying pan and soften the sage leaves and thyme.

8   Sprinkle the ravioli with grated Parmesan and pour over the strained butter.

Fazzoletti with asparagus

Preparation: 1 hour
   10 minutes

350 g/12 oz small green
   asparagus
salt, 1 tbsp olive oil
4 tbsp grated Parmesan
pepper
12 marrow flowers
1 small courgette
80 g/3 oz butter

225 g/8 oz fazzoletti

To make the pasta:
200 g/7 oz flour
2 eggs
salt

For the sauce:
50 g/2 oz butter
40 g/1½ oz flour
250 ml/½ pint milk
nutmeg

Fazzoletti are thin
"handkerchief" sheets of
pasta normally served with
delicate sauces and
accompaniments. If you
wish to buy them but find
they are unavailable, thin
lasagna sheets could be
substituted.

1 Trim and rinse the asparagus. Cut off the green tips and cook the stems in boiling salted water for about 15 minutes.

2 Drain the stems and purée in a blender.

3 Cook the asparagus tips in boiling salted water for about 10 minutes.

4 Prepare a sheet of pasta* and cut into eight 10-cm/4-in squares. Cook the fazzoletti in plenty of boiling salted water for 3-5 minutes, adding 1 tbsp oil to prevent them from sticking together.

5 Melt 50 g/2 oz butter in a small saucepan, add the flour and stir for 1 minute. Add the hot milk and a pinch of nutmeg and cook for about 15 minutes.

6 Add the asparagus purée and season lightly with salt.

7 Place a fazzoletto in each of four dishes; arrange the asparagus tips on top, pointing outward. Sprinkle with grated Parmesan and pepper. Place three marrow flowers on top and cover with a little sauce. Cover with a second square of pasta.

8 Garnish each dish with a few slices of courgette, sautéed in 25 g/1 oz butter, and two asparagus tips. Transfer to a preheated oven, at 170°C/325°F/mark 3, for a few minutes. Pour 1 tablespoon melted butter over each dish before serving.

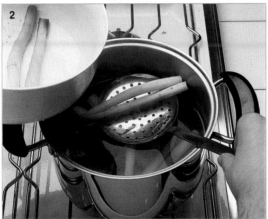

Tortelli with pumpkin

Preparation: 1³/₄ hours

800 g/1³/₄ lb pumpkin
50 g/2 oz macaroons
 (amaretti)
100 g/3¹/₂ oz sweet fruit
 pickle
4 tbsp grated Parmesan
nutmeg
salt and pepper
125 g/4 oz butter

For the pasta:
250 g/9 oz flour
3 eggs
salt

1 Cut the pumpkin into slices and discard the seeds. Remove the rind and bake the slices in the oven for 20 minutes.

2 Press the pumpkin through a fine sieve with the back of a wooden spoon.

3 Crush the macaroons and mix with the minced sweet fruit pickle, 2 tablespoons grated Parmesan and a pinch of nutmeg. Season with salt and pepper and stir well.

4 Prepare a sheet of pasta dough* and roll out into two layers. Using a knife score the bottom sheet into twenty 10-cm/4-in squares. Place a ball of filling in the centre of each square.

5 Cover with the second sheet of dough; press round the edges of each square to seal, then cut out the tortelli with a pastry wheel.

6 Cook the tortelli in boiling salted water for 2 minutes.

7 Remove them one at a time from the saucepan, using a slotted spoon. Drain and place on warmed plates.

8 Sprinkle with grated Parmesan and spoon over the melted butter.

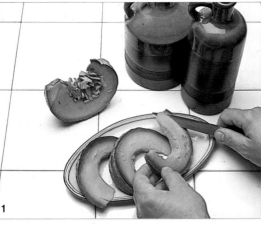

Spinach gnocchetti with leeks and beans

Preparation: 2 hours
40 minutes (+ 12 hours
for soaking the beans)

175 g/6 oz cannellini beans
salt and pepper
275 g/10 oz potatoes
225 g/8 oz spinach
2 egg yolks
125 g/4 oz flour
nutmeg
8 leeks
100 g/3¹/₂ oz butter
4 fresh basil leaves
4 fresh sage leaves
225 ml/8 fl oz white wine
4 tbsp meat stock
    (preferably veal)

1 Soak the beans in cold
water for 12 hours; drain,
then cook in boiling salted
water for 1¹/₄ hours. Skin
and boil the potatoes, then
mash them.

2 Cook the rinsed spinach
for 5-7 minutes until tender.
Drain well and mince in a
food processor.

3 Mix the chopped
spinach with the potatoes;
add the egg yolks, flour, a
pinch of nutmeg and salt
and work together until well
blended.

4 Break off pieces of the
mixture and roll into
sausages the thickness of
your finger; cut into
gnocchetti.

5 Cut the leeks into
4-cm/1¹/₂-in pieces and fry
gently in a frying pan in
50 g/2 oz butter. Add the
basil, sage and white wine
and simmer gently. Add the
beans with a little of their
cooking liquid and the meat
stock. Simmer for a few
minutes.

6 Cook the gnocchetti in
boiling salted water for 2-3
minutes. Drain, season with
pepper and sauté briefly in
the remaining butter. Serve
in very hot dishes with the
beans and leeks and a little
of the cooking liquid from
the vegetables.

Gazpacho

Preparation: 40 minutes

2 slices bread
6 tbsp red wine vinegar
1 small cucumber
1 red pepper
2 cloves garlic
1 large onion
225 ml/8 fl oz olive oil
700 g/1¹/₂ lb ripe plum
   tomatoes
salt
pepper

To serve:
1 red pepper, diced
1 cucumber, diced
croûtons
12 small onions
2 hard-boiled eggs

1   Soak the bread in the vinegar for a few hours.

2   Into a blender place the soaked bread, the peeled and roughly chopped cucumber, 1 seeded and chopped red pepper, the garlic, the peeled and sliced onion, 6 tbsp olive oil and ¹/₂ litre/1 pint water. Blend until smooth and then pour into a bowl.

3   Skin and seed the tomatoes then mash to a pulp. Add to the puréed vegetable mixture, season with salt and pepper and refrigerate.

4   Serve the gazpacho with ice cubes, and bowls of diced red pepper, diced cucumber, small onions, hard-boiled eggs and croûtons.

Vichyssoise

Preparation: 1 hour
  (+ chilling time)

6 large leeks
225 g/8 oz potatoes
50 g/2 oz butter
white pepper
salt
1 bouquet garni
175 ml/6 fl oz single cream
chicken stock
chives

1   Trim the leeks and cut the white part into rings, keeping some of the green for garnish. Peel and dice the potatoes.

2   Melt the butter and sauté the leeks without letting them brown. Add the potatoes and stir well to coat. Season with pepper.

3   Cook for a few minutes, then add 1½ litres/2½ pints water. Add salt to taste and the bouquet garni and bring to the boil. Lower the heat and simmer for about 40 minutes, half covered.

4   Purée in a blender, return to the saucepan and add the cream and a little chicken stock as required. Reheat gently but do not allow to boil. Cool then refrigerate for at least 1 hour.

5   Serve chilled, garnished with chopped chives and a few green leek rings.

Country-style chickpea soup

Preparation: 3 hours

450 g/1 lb chickpeas
400 g/14 oz greens
¹/₂ onion
3 tbsp oil
200 g/7 oz pork rind,
    chopped
225 ml/8 fl oz freshly made
    tomato sauce*
2 tbsp grated Parmesan
few slices toasted bread

1   Soak the chickpeas for 12 hours. Drain, then bring to the boil in fresh, unsalted water. Simmer for 2 hours.

2   Trim the greens and shred the leaves, reserving the stalks. Fry the chopped onion in the oil in a saucepan, then add the pork rind, tomato sauce, shredded leaves and salt to taste; cook over a medium heat for 1 hour, adding 1¹/₂ litres/2¹/₂ pints water.

3   Add the chickpeas and the chopped stalks. Cook for another hour.

4   Serve sprinkled with grated Parmesan and black pepper. Accompany with slices of toasted bread.

Italian minestrone

Preparation: 1 hour
40 minutes

2 medium carrots
2 stalks celery
1 head lettuce
4 leaves Savoy cabbage
$^1/_2$ cauliflower
2 potatoes
3 tbsp oil
salt and pepper
2 tbsp tomato purée
2 stock cubes
1 bunch parsley
sprig rosemary
2 cloves garlic
175 g/6 oz small pasta (e.g.
   ditalini)
2 tbsp grated Parmesan

1   Shred the lettuce and cabbage. Cut the cauliflower into florets. Peel and slice the carrots; chop the celery and dice the potatoes.

2   Heat the oil in a large saucepan over a low heat, then sauté the vegetables for 10 minutes, stirring occasionally. Season with pepper; add the tomato purée and $1^1/_2$ litres/ $2^1/_2$ pints water.

3   Crumble the stock cubes into the soup; adjust the seasoning and cook for about $1^1/_4$ hours.

4   Chop the herbs and the peeled garlic. Add to the soup, together with the pasta, and cook until *al dente*. Add the Parmesan before serving.

Stuffed onions

Preparation: 2 hours

25 g/1 oz dried mushrooms
4 large white onions
1 red pepper
2 tbsp oil
salt and pepper
2 tbsp breadcrumbs
1 cup grated Emmental
   cheese
40 g/1½ oz butter

1   Soak the mushrooms in warm water for 20 minutes. Squeeze out and chop.

2   Peel the onions, cover with water and boil for 15 minutes. Drain, cook, then cut off the top; scoop out and reserve the middle. Dice the pepper.

3   Chop the middles of the onions and sauté in the oil. Add the red pepper and the mushrooms. Season. Cover and simmer for 10 minutes. Remove from the heat and add the breadcrumbs. Stir.

4   Stuff the onions with the mixture and place in a buttered ovenproof dish. Sprinkle with grated Emmental and melted butter. Bake at 180°C/ 350°F/mark 4 for 50 minutes, covering with foil if they begin to brown too much. Serve hot.

Vegetable moulds

Preparation: 1 hour

2 carrots
2 courgettes
1 large aubergine
1 large red pepper
125 g/4 oz grated Parmesan
3 tbsp milk or cream
2 bunches fresh basil
250 g/9 oz plum tomatoes
  (or tinned)
3 eggs
5 tbsp oil
butter
salt and pepper

1   Dice the carrots. Cut the courgettes and aubergine into medium pieces. Using a fork, hold the pepper over a flame until the skin blisters, then rinse under cold running water and rub off the skin. Chop.

2   Boil a small amount of water in two separate saucepans. Add the carrots to one and the courgettes and aubergine to the other, and cook for about 15 minutes, adding the pepper to the carrots for the last few minutes. Drain, cool, then place in a blender with the milk (or cream), 3 tablespoons oil, the eggs and grated cheese. Blend until smooth. Add salt to taste, then divide the mixture between four buttered moulds. Place in a bain-marie and bake at 190°C/375°F/mark 5 for about 20 minutes.

3   Peel and chop the tomatoes, blend with the basil, and a few tablespoons oil. Season.

4   Remove the moulds from the oven and allow to cool. Unmould on to serving dishes on a layer of tomato sauce. Serve the remaining sauce separately.

Stuffed cabbage leaves

 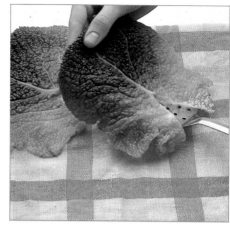 

Preparation: 1 hour
30 minutes

275 g/10 oz potatoes, peeled
8 Savoy cabbage leaves
salt
50 g/2 oz butter
100 ml/4 fl oz milk
50 g/2 oz grated Parmesan
pepper
nutmeg
50 g/2 oz cooked ham
1 bunch parsley
1 egg
1 tbsp breadcrumbs

1   Boil the potatoes for 20 minutes. Cut the central rib away from the cabbage leaves and discard.

2   Cook the cabbage leaves in salted water for 5 minutes, then dry on a tea towel.

3   Mash the potatoes.

4   Add half the butter, the milk and half the cheese. Season with salt, pepper and grated nutmeg. Stir over a low heat until the mixture is quite dry, then remove from the heat and add the chopped ham and parsley. Stir in the egg and breadcrumbs; mix well and adjust the seasoning.

5   Place a cabbage leaf on a chopping board, overlapping the edges of the cut, and place one eighth of the mixture in the centre.

6   Fold the edges of the leaf over toward the centre to make a parcel. Fill all the leaves and place in a buttered ovenproof dish. Sprinkle with the remaining melted butter and cheese and cook at 200°C/400°F/ mark 6 for 15-20 minutes.

Courgette layer

Preparation: 40 minutes

125 g/4 oz parsley
3 anchovy fillets in oil
2 cloves garlic
1 tbsp vinegar
125 ml/4 fl oz olive oil
salt and pepper
1 hard-boiled egg
6 medium courgettes
flour
oil for frying

1   Chop the parsley, anchovy fillets and garlic. Mix in a bowl, adding the vinegar, olive oil, salt and pepper.

3   Chop the hard-boiled egg finely and add to the sauce.

4   Slice the courgettes lengthwise and coat lightly in flour. Fry in plenty of hot oil until just brown. Drain on kitchen paper.

6   Arrange in layers on a serving dish, sprinkling each layer with a little salt and some sauce, and chill for 2-3 hours before serving.

Leeks with herb sauce

Preparation: 1 hour

1¹/₂ lemons
3 parsley stalks
2 shallots
12 white peppercorns
1 tbsp cumin seeds
6 coriander seeds
1 bay leaf
8 medium leeks
3 egg yolks
1 150 g/5 oz carton yoghurt
salt
1 tsp mustard
few drops Worcestershire
  sauce
few chives

1   Place 250 ml/9 fl oz water and the juice of 1 lemon in a saucepan with the parsley, the chopped shallots, peppercorns, cumin, coriander and bay leaf; boil for a few minutes.

2   Cut the leeks to equal lengths and rinse well. Place in a saucepan and pour over the filtered stock. Cover and cook over a low heat for 15 minutes.

3   In a bowl beat the egg yolks, yoghurt and juice of ¹/₂ lemon. Cook in a bain-marie for 10-12 minutes, stirring and adjusting the seasoning as necessary. Remove from the heat and stir in the mustard, Worcestershire sauce and a sprinkling of pepper.

4   Drain the leeks; arrange on a serving dish and cover with the sauce. Garnish with chopped chives.

Cucumber and crisp cabbage salad

Preparation: 1 hour

2 small cucumbers
2 tsp salt
3-4 cabbage leaves

For the sauce:
1 tsp soy sauce
1 tbsp hot black bean paste
(available from Oriental
stores)
few drops sesame seed oil

1   Trim the ends off the
cucumbers diagonally and
slice diagonally into thin
pieces. Sprinkle the slices
with 1 tsp salt and leave to
stand for a few minutes.

2   Cut out the hard ribs of
the cabbage, wash and then
cut into small pieces
4-5 cm/1^{1}/$_{2}$-2 in long;
sprinkle with 1 tsp salt and
leave to stand.

3   When the cucumber and
cabbage slices have
softened a little, rinse off the
salt and drain.

4   Mix all the sauce
ingredients thoroughly
together in a bowl, add the
cucumber and cabbage
pieces, stir well and leave
the vegetables to absorb the
sauce before serving.

Bamboo shoots with spinach and mushrooms

Approximately 450 g/1 lb
   fresh spinach
100 g/3¹/₂ oz bamboo shoots
4-5 Chinese mushrooms
oil for frying
1 tsp salt
225 ml/8 fl oz water
1 tbsp oyster sauce
few drops sesame oil
1 tsp cornflour dissolved in 2
   tsp water

1   Wash the spinach; pat
dry and chop.

2   Boil the bamboo shoots
until tender and slice thinly.

3   Soak the mushrooms in
water for 20 minutes, if they
are dried; remove the stems
and cut the larger caps in
half.

4   Heat 1¹/₂ tablespoons oil
in a wok, stir-fry the spinach
briefly and then add the salt
and water. Cover and cook
over a low heat until tender;
drain.

5   Clean the wok and heat
1¹/₂ tablespoons of fresh oil;
when very hot, add the
bamboo shoots and the
mushrooms and stir-fry.

6   When nearly done, add
the spinach, stock and
oyster sauce, finishing with a
few drops of sesame oil.

7   Cover and cook for 2 to
3 minutes. Thicken the
sauce by stirring in 1
teaspoon cornflour mixed
with 2 teaspoons water.

Vegetable pie

Preparation: 1 hour 10
   minutes

225 g/8 oz frozen puff pastry
125 g/4 oz carrots
2 small onions
50 g/2 oz butter
225 g/8 oz peas
175 g/6 oz spinach, cooked
   and chopped
salt
350 g/12 oz ricotta
2 eggs
50 g/2 oz grated Parmesan
6 tbsp milk
flour

1   Thaw the pastry at room
temperature. Boil the carrots
and slice the onions.

2   Fry the onion in
50 g/2 oz butter for 5
minutes, then add the peas,
carrots and spinach. Season.

3   Transfer to a bowl; add
the crumbled ricotta, *eggs*,
grated cheese and milk.
Season again.

4   Divide the pastry in two;
roll out and cut two circles,
one slightly larger than the
other. Butter and flour a
springform pie tin and line
with the larger pastry circle.
Prick the surface.

5   Pour in the filling and
cover with the second pastry
circle.

6   Cook in a hot oven
(200°C/400°F/mark 6) for
40 minutes.

Fennel au gratin

Preparation: 50 minutes

900 g/2 lb fennel
salt
175 g/6 oz cooked ham
6 slices cheese
15 g/¹/₂ oz butter
2 tbsp grated Parmesan
1 tbsp chopped parsley
25 g/1 oz butter
25 g/1 oz flour
225 ml/8 fl oz milk
salt
pepper
pinch nutmeg

1 Cut each fennel bulb lengthwise into eight. Cook in boiling salted water for 5 minutes. Cut the ham and cheese into strips.

2 Butter a baking dish and arrange alternate strips of fennel, ham and cheese in a wheel. Sprinkle with a little grated cheese and chopped parsley.

3 Melt the butter in a saucepan. Stir in the flour and cook for 1 minute. Gradually stir in the milk, mixing well over a low heat until thick. Season with salt, pepper and nutmeg. Pour the sauce over the fennel, sprinkle with the remaining cheese and cook at 200°C/400°F/mark 6 for about 25 minutes until crisp and brown.

Baked aubergines

Preparation: 1 hour
     30 minutes

2 large aubergines
salt and pepper
150 g/5 oz minced beef
50 g/2 oz pork
50 g/2 oz sausage
1 egg yolk
1 tbsp chopped parsley
4 tbsp grated Parmesan
oil for frying
50 g/2 oz butter

1   Slice the aubergines. Sprinkle with salt and leave in a colander for 1 hour to drain away the bitter juices. In a blender or food processor blend the minced beef, pork and skinned sausage. Transfer to a bowl and mix in the egg yolk, chopped parsley and 2 tablespoons Parmesan. Season.

2   Fry the aubergines in plenty of oil until tender. Drain on kitchen paper.

3   Place a little meat mixture on eight aubergine slices then cover each one with another slice, pressing lightly. Place in a single layer in a buttered ovenproof dish. Sprinkle with 2 tablespoons Parmesan and a few pieces of butter. Bake at 200°C/400°F/mark 6 for 35 minutes.

Savoury potato croquettes

Preparation: 1 hour
        10 minutes

900 g/2 lb potatoes
salt
1 medium onion
oil
450 g/1 lb shelled peas
¹/₂ stock cube
40 g/1¹/₂ oz butter
4 eggs, separated
3 tbsp grated Parmesan
50 g/2 oz cooked ham
flour

1   Boil and mash the potatoes. Chop the onion and fry briefly in 1¹/₂ tablespoons oil. Add the peas and the crumbled stock cube; cover and simmer over a low heat for 20 minutes, stirring occasionally and adding a little water as necessary.

2   Stir the butter into the cooled potatoes, 4 egg yolks, the Parmesan, chopped ham, peas and a pinch of salt. Mix well.

3   Turn the mixture on to a work surface and shape into croquettes.

4   Beat 2 egg whites with 1 tablespoon oil. Coat the croquettes lightly with flour, then dip in the egg white mixture. Fry a few at a time in plenty of hot oil.

Potato bake

Preparation: 1 hour

900 g/2 lb potatoes
4 tbsp oil
80 g/3 oz grated Parmesan
50 g/2 oz grated Emmental
   cheese
salt
pepper
25 g/1 oz butter

1   Peel the potatoes, then grate them using a hand grater or food processor. Mix in a bowl with the oil, 50 g/2 oz grated Parmesan and 25 g/1 oz grated Emmental. Season.

2   Butter an ovenproof baking dish and pour in the potato mixture. Smooth the surface and sprinkle with the remaining cheese and a few pieces of butter.

3   Bake at 220°C/425°F/ mark 7 for about 30 minutes until golden brown.

Carrot ring cake

For the dough:
225 g/8 oz carrots
50 g/2 oz sugar
3 egg yolks
65 g/2¹/₂ oz plain flour
50 g/2 oz ground almonds
1 tsp grated lemon peel
1 tbsp lemon juice
2 tbsp orange liqueur
butter to grease and flour to
   dust mould

For the buttercream:
25 g/1 oz icing sugar
50 g/1 oz butter
1 egg yolk
1 tbsp kirsch

This recipe is a variation of
one of the most famous
types of carrot cake, made in
the canton of Aargau in
Switzerland. It is sometimes
covered with chocolate
icing. The Aargau carrot
cake is covered with kirsch-
flavoured icing and is
decorated with chopped,
toasted almonds, then
sprinkled with icing sugar.

1   Butter and flour a ring mould.

2   Peel and grate the carrots.

3   Place the sugar, egg yolks and flour in a bowl over hot water and whisk until the mixture thickens.

4   Remove from the heat and stir in the carrots, ground almonds, grated lemon peel and lemon juice.

5   Whip the egg whites until stiff.

6   Fold carefully into the carrot mixture.

7   Pour half the mixture into the mould. Prepare the kirsch-flavoured buttercream* and spread over the surface, then cover with the remaining mixture.

8   Bake in a preheated oven at 180°C/350°F/mark 4 for 45 minutes. Unmould and brush the top with Cointreau. Decorate with Chantilly cream*.

Fruit

Hawaiian fruit salad

$^1/_2$ fresh pineapple
2 bananas
juice of $^1/_2$ lemon
2 kiwi fruit
1 mango
3 or 4 lettuce leaves
1 orange or mandarin,
  peeled, segmented
10 maraschino cherries,
  drained
2 tbsp sugar

Orange cream:
100 ml/4 fl oz orange juice
50 g/2 oz sugar
1 egg yolk, beaten
150 ml/5 fl oz whipping cream

Fruit salads are often served with whipping cream or sweet liqueur, such as Marsala, maraschino or kirsch. This one has an unusual cream dressing. Some more elaborate fruit salads can be garnished with yoghurt, cream cheese, chopped toasted nuts or whole nuts, such as pine nuts.

1   Drain off the juice from the pineapple half.

2   Remove the hard core from the half pineapple. Cut all round the flesh of the pineapple so that it can be removed in chunks with a teaspoon.

3   Lay the empty pineapple half cut side down on a cloth to drain the fruit of the remaining juice.

4   Peel and slice the bananas and sprinkle with the lemon juice.

5   Peel and slice the kiwi fruit.

6   Peel the mango, remove the stone and cut the fruit into pieces.

7   Arrange the lettuce leaves in the pineapple half and fill with the drained fruit pieces; add the mandarins in sections and the cherries. Sprinkle with sugar.

8   To make the orange cream, place the orange juice in a saucepan, add the sugar and dissolve over a low heat. Remove from the heat. Beat the egg yolk in a bowl with a metal whisk and add to the orange mixture. Stir over a very low heat until the custard thickens. Allow to cool completely. Whip the cream and stir into the orange sauce. Chill the cream in the refrigerator and pour over the fruit salad just before serving.

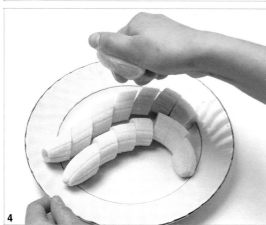

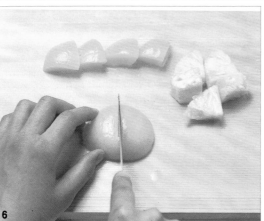

Baked apple

Serves 1

1 large baking apple
1 tbsp apricot jam or peach
    jam
1 shortbread biscuit or
    macaroon, crumbled
1 tsp butter
sliced almonds
1 tsp sugar
5 tbsp Marsala or port

1   Wash and dry the apple.
Remove the core. With a
sharp knife cut a circle right
round the apple. Place in a
buttered baking dish.

2   Mix the jam with the
crumbled biscuit and stir
until smooth; fill the centre
of the apple with this
mixture.

3   Dot the top of the apple
with butter and with sliced
almonds.

4   Sprinkle the apple with
the sugar; this will form a
crust when the apple is
cooked.

5   Pour the Marsala or port
into the baking dish and
bake the apple in the top
part of the oven, preheated
to 180°C/350°F/mark 4 for
30 minutes.

Turkish oranges

Serves 6

6 oranges
water
350 g/12 oz sugar
2 cloves

1   Peel the oranges thinly, taking care not to cut away the pith with the rind. Cut the peel into very thin strips.

2   Cover the peel with cold water, bring to the boil and drain when the peel is tender.

3   Place the sugar, 25 ml/ 4 fl oz of water and the cloves in a saucepan and heat gently until the mixture begins to caramelise.

4   Add the shredded peel and 60 ml/2 fl oz water and stir until the peel is coated with syrup. Leave to cool slightly.

5   Carefully spoon the syrup and caramelised peel over the oranges, turning them so that they are evenly covered with syrup and peel.

6   Chill the oranges in the refrigerator for several hours. Before serving, quarter the oranges from top to bottom.

Glazed fresh fruit

glacé icing or liqueur-
    flavoured glacé icing*
fresh fruit of choice

Choose your liqueur
according to the fruit you are
using. For example, use
brandy with grapes and
kirsch, cherry brandy or
maraschino with cherries.

1   Wash the fruit and dry
carefully with a clean cloth.

2   Dip the fruit into the
glaze and allow the glaze to
harden.

Almond-filled dried fruit and nuts

almond paste*
food colouring (optional)
dried dates, prunes,
   apricots, peaches or other
   dried fruit
halved walnuts, pecans,
   almonds or other nuts

1   Remove the stones from the dates and prunes, cutting the fruit in half or leaving the two halves slightly joined. Fill with the almond paste.

2   For the nuts, divide the kernel in half and sandwich the two halves together with the almond paste (plain or coloured with food colouring). You can also dip stuffed dried fruit and nuts into melted chocolate and allow the chocolate to harden.

Banana crêpes

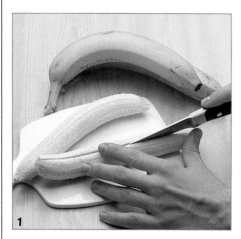

Preparation: 1 hour
(+ 2 hours for resting the
batter)

4 ripe bananas
1 lemon
drop vanilla essence
1 tsp sugar
150 ml/5 fl oz brandy
2 eggs
salt
125 g/4 oz flour
250 ml/9 fl oz milk
50 g/2 oz butter
1 tbsp sugar

1   Peel the bananas and
cut in half lengthwise.
Sprinkle with lemon juice.

2   Mix together the vanilla,
1 teaspoon sugar and 2
tablespoons brandy. Stir
well.

3   Pour over the bananas;
leave to stand.

4   Beat the eggs in a
bowl with a pinch of salt;
gradually stir in the flour and
then the cold milk. Add
15 g/^{1}/$_2$ oz melted butter and
2 tbsp brandy. Leave to
stand for 2 hours, then make
8 crêpes.

5   Wrap each half banana
in a crêpe and place on a
serving dish.

6   Heat 4 tablespoons
brandy with 1 tablespoon
sugar in a small saucepan.
Flame and pour over the
crêpes.

Fruit salad and cream

900 g/2 lb assorted fresh or
    tinned fruit
125 g/4 oz sugar
few drops vanilla essence
juice of 1 lemon
2-3 tbsp rum or maraschino
400 ml/14 fl oz single cream
50 g/2 oz chopped dried fruit
20-30 g/1 oz chopped nuts

1   Wash, drain and peel the
fresh fruit. Slice the fresh
and the tinned fruit.

2   Place together with the
dried fruit in a large serving
bowl.

3   Mix together the sugar,
vanilla essence, lemon juice
and liqueur. Pour over the
fruit salad and stir.

4   Pour over the cream and
scatter the chopped nuts on
top.

5   Leave to stand in a cool
place for several hours
before serving.

Melon Portuguese

1 1-kg/2-lb cantaloupe or
  honeydew melon
50 g/2 oz sugar
¹/₂ tsp ground cinnamon
200 ml/7 fl oz white port
Chantilly cream*

1   With the stalk
uppermost, cut a zigzag ring
round the melon and
remove the top. Scoop out
the seeds.

2   Remove the flesh from
the melon using a melon
scoop.

3   Replace the balls of
melon in the shell; add sugar
and cinnamon and leave to
stand for 15 minutes.

4   Add the port and place
in the refrigerator for 1 hour.

5   Serve with Chantilly
cream. This fruit salad is
served in the melon shell. It
can be prepared in various
ways. Add soft fruits of your
choice and a sprinkling of
pistachios, use kirsch or
maraschino liqueur instead
of port wine, or add other
mixed fruits to melon. Top
with vanilla ice cream and
brandy. Or add pineapple,
bananas and kirsch.

Peach Melba

300 g/10 oz fresh raspberries
  or 1 (225 g/8 oz) jar
  raspberry jelly
2-4 tbsp warm water
200 g/7 oz icing sugar
3 tbsp lemon juice
$\frac{1}{8}$ tsp vanilla essence
2-3 tbsp raspberry liqueur
6 fresh peaches, peeled,
  halved or 12 tinned peach
  halves
175 g/6 oz caster sugar
$\frac{1}{2}$ litre/18 fl oz water
700 g/1$\frac{1}{2}$ lb vanilla ice
  cream

1   Purée the raspberries
with the water in a blender.
If you are using jelly, heat it
gently with a little water.

2   In a large bowl mix
together the raspberry
purée, sugar, lemon juice,
vanilla essence and liqueur.
Place in the refrigerator for 1
hour.

3   Place a layer of ice
cream in the bottom of 6
glasses or dishes; place 2
peach halves on the ice
cream. (If the peaches are
fresh they should be
prepared in the following
way: boil $\frac{1}{2}$ litre/18 fl oz
water with 175g/6oz sugar
and simmer the peaches in
this syrup for not more than
5 minutes.) Add 2 scoops of
ice cream and pour over the
purée.

Pears in white wine

3 large pears
125 g/4 oz sugar
150 ml/5 fl oz white wine
150 ml/5 fl oz water
strip of lemon peel
2 whole cloves

1   Peel the pears, cut them in half and remove the cores.

2   Place the pears in a saucepan with the remaining ingredients (reserving half the wine) over a moderate heat.

3   Simmer until the pears are tender.

4   Drain the pears and place on a serving dish.

5   Add the remaining wine to the cooking liquid. Bring to the boil, lower the heat and simmer for 5-10 minutes.

6   Remove the cloves and lemon peel. Pour the syrup over the pears and allow to cool before serving.

Kiwi bavarois

Preparation: 1 hour
    30 minutes

600 g/1¼ lb sugar
5 kiwi fruit
1 lemon
400 ml/14 fl oz double
    cream
½ stick vanilla
4 egg yolks
2 level tbsp powdered
    gelatine
2 tbsp apricot jelly
grated coconut

1   Make a syrup by boiling 1 litre/1¾ pints water and 450 g/1 lb sugar. Peel the kiwi fruit; cut them in half, sprinkle with the lemon juice, then leave to stand in the hot syrup for 10 minutes.

2   Gently heat 325 g/11 oz cream with the vanilla; heat 50 g/2 oz sugar in a small saucepan until it caramelises.

3   Pour the caramel into the warm cream and stir. Sift, return to the heat and bring to the boil. Remove from the heat.

4   Beat the egg yolks with 50 g/2 oz sugar until creamy. Gradually stir in the caramel cream mixture. Prepare the gelatine according to the manufacturer's instructions and stir into the cream mixture, stirring over a very low heat until it thickens and the gelatine is dissolved. Leave to cool. Whip the remaining cream and fold into the cooled bavarois.

5   Line a mould with foil. Cut the kiwi fruit into rings and place in the bottom.

6   Cover with the bavarois and chill for a few hours. Unmould and brush the top with warmed apricot jelly. Sprinkle with grated coconut.

Chestnut tart

1 kg/2¼ lb chestnut flour
150 ml/5 fl oz vegetable oil
1 tbsp sugar
½ tsp salt
125 g/4 oz pine nuts
175 g/6 oz sultanas
225 ml/8 fl oz water
1 sprig rosemary

Chestnut tart or *castagnaccio* is an Italian speciality, from the rural part of northern Tuscany. It can be served hot or cold, though its subtle flavour is more fully appreciated when it is eaten hot.

1   In a large bowl mix together the chestnut flour, oil, sugar, salt, three quarters of the pine nuts and three quarters of the sultanas. Add enough water to make a soft batter of pouring consistency.

2   Pour the mixture into a large, low-sided cake tin which has been brushed with oil: the paste should not be more than 2-2.5 cm/³⁄₄-1 in thick.

3   Brush the surface with oil. Sprinkle with the remaining pine nuts, sultanas and the rosemary.

4   Cook in a preheated oven at 200°C/400°F/mark 6 for 1 hour.

5   Before serving transfer to a serving dish.

Quick apple cake

6 cooking apples
juice of $^1/_2$ lemon
50 g/2 oz sugar

For the dough:
50 g/2 oz butter or
 margarine
125 g/4 oz sugar
2 egg yolks
juice of $^1/_2$ lemon
grated peel of $^1/_2$ lemon
125 g/4 oz plain flour
1 tsp baking powder
125 ml/4 fl oz milk
2 tbsp rum
3 egg whites

For the glaze:
25 g/1 oz butter or
 margarine, melted
1 egg yolk

1   Peel the apples and use
an apple corer or a sharp
knife to remove the cores.

2   Sprinkle the apples with
lemon juice and sugar and
put to one side.

3   Cream the butter and
sugar. Beat in the egg yolks,
the juice of half a lemon and
the grated lemon peel.

4   Sift the flour and baking
powder together and add to
the mixture together with
the milk and rum.

5   Whisk the egg whites
and fold them carefully into
the mixture, stirring from
bottom to top.

6   Pour the mixture into a
buttered cake tin or
ovenproof dish. Press the
apples into the mixture.
Brush the cake generously
with melted butter and
beaten egg yolk.

7   Bake in a preheated
oven at 170°C/325°F/mark
3 for 35-40 minutes.

8   Remove from the oven
and sprinkle with icing sugar
if desired.

Fruit soufflé omelette

Preparation: 40 minutes

4 eggs, separated
80 g/3 oz vanilla sugar
2 tbsp flour
1 tbsp lemon juice
salt
25 g/1 oz butter
225 g/8 oz raspberries
icing sugar
2 tbsp rum

1   Beat the egg yolks and vanilla sugar until pale and creamy. Sift the flour and gradually stir into the beaten eggs.

2   Whisk the egg whites with the lemon juice and a pinch of salt until stiff. Fold into the egg yolks using a metal spoon.

3   Heat the butter in a non-stick baking pan and pour in the soufflé omelette mixture. Heat gently for 5-6 minutes until the bottom is golden brown. Transfer to a hot oven (240°C/475°F/mark 9) for 3 minutes. Pour the raspberries into the centre and leave in the oven for 1 minute.

4   Slide the omelette on to a serving dish and fold in half. Sprinkle with icing sugar.

5   Heat the rum in a small saucepan; pour over the omelette and flame. Serve at once.

Papaya cups

Preparation: 20 minutes

2 small papaya
3 kiwi fruit
6 tbsp rum
120 ml/4 fl oz whipping
   cream
2 tbsp icing sugar

1   Cut the papaya lengthwise in half and scoop out and discard the black seeds in the middle. Spoon out the flesh and cut into medium-size pieces. Put the empty skins in the freezer.

2   Peel the kiwi fruit and chop. Place all the fruit in a bowl, sprinkle with rum and leave to stand for 1 hour.

3   Just before serving, whip the cream with the icing sugar and spoon into a piping bag.

4   Spoon the fruit with a little of the juice into the reserved papaya skins; decorate with the whipped cream.

Summer fruit jelly

Preparation: 30 minutes
(+ chilling time)

600 g/1¼ lb mixed summer
fruit (strawberries,
raspberries, bilberries,
blackberries, redcurrants)
200 g/7 oz sugar
2 level tbsp powdered
gelatine
2 tbsp kirsch
juice of 1 lemon

1   Place one third of the
fruit with the sugar in a
saucepan and simmer over a
low heat for 10 minutes.
Strain, then pour the syrup
into a saucepan.

2   Prepare the gelatine
according to the
manufacturer's instructions,
then add to the syrup. Stir
over a low heat until the
gelatine is dissolved. Turn
off the heat and immediately
stir in the kirsch and lemon
juice.

3   Rinse four individual
moulds in water, then pour a
little syrup into the bottom of
each. Divide the remaining
fruit between the moulds.
Cover with the syrup and
refrigerate for several hours.

4   Dip briefly into hot water
to unmould.

Tropical jelly mould

Preparation: 30 minutes
 (+ chilling time)

600 ml/1 pint orange juice
2 level tbsp powdered
 gelatine
1 450-g/1-lb mango
200 g/7 oz pineapple slices
200 g/7 oz tinned lychees
140 ml/5 fl oz whipping
 cream
50 g/¹/₂ oz icing sugar
grated peel of 2 oranges

1   Sift the orange juice.
Prepare the gelatine
according to the
manufacturer's instructions,
dissolving it in 3 tablespoons
orange juice, then adding
the remaining orange juice
once it has dissolved.

2   Rinse a 25-cm/10-in ring
mould in cold water and
pour in a layer of gelatine.
Place in the freezer.

3   Place the remaining
gelatine in the refrigerator.
Chop the mango and
pineapple and quarter the
lychees.

4   As soon as the gelatine
begins to set, stir in the fruit
and pour into the mould.
Refrigerate for at least 3
hours.

5   Whip the cream with the
icing sugar, and add the
orange peel.

6   Dip the mould briefly in
hot water, then turn out.
Decorate with the whipped
cream.

Desserts and Cakes

Snow cake

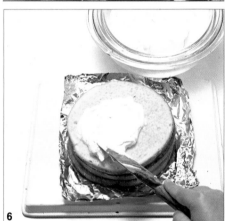

1 sponge cake*
brandy
225 ml/8 fl oz milk
50 g/2 oz sugar
2 egg yolks
juice and grated peel of 1
  orange
1¹/₂ tbsp Curaçao
3 tbsp Grand Marnier
Chantilly cream* (basic
  recipe +¹/₂)

1 Heat the milk and sugar gently to dissolve the sugar but do not allow to boil. Leave to cool slightly.

2 Beat the egg yolks. Add the milk and sugar from step 1.

3 Return this mixture to the saucepan and stir constantly. Remove from the heat just before boiling point is reached. The custard should have thickened sufficiently to coat the back of a spoon.

4 Add the orange juice and grated peel, the Curaçao and 1¹/₂ tbsp of Grand Marnier.

5 Cut the sponge into three layers. Sprinkle with the remaining Grand Marnier. Sandwich the layers with the custard filling.

6 Pipe the Chantilly cream flavoured with brandy on the top of the cake.

Coffee cream cake

For the sponge:
175 g/6 oz sugar
6 eggs, separated
175 g/6 oz plain flour
few drops vanilla essence
coffee liqueur
butter to grease and flour to
  dust tin

For the coffee buttercream:
200 g/7 oz butter
175 g/6 oz icing sugar
2 egg yolks
2 tbsp strong black coffee
few drops vanilla essence

For decoration:
80 g/3 oz toasted sliced
  almonds
1 tbsp cocoa powder

1   Beat together the sugar and egg yolks, standing the bowl over a bowl of hot water.

2   Whip the egg whites until stiff and fold gently into the sugar and egg yolk mixture.

3   Sift the flour and fold with the vanilla essence into the mixture.

4   Butter a 20-cm/8-in springform tin and dust with flour. Pour the mixture into the tin. Place in a preheated oven at 170°C/325°F/mark 3 for 40 minutes.

5   For the buttercream make a sugar syrup with the icing sugar and a little water, allow it to cool, then add it to the egg yolks.

6   Cream the butter and stir in the mixture from step 5. Add the coffee, and mix again.

7   Cut the sponge into three equal layers. Using a pastry brush, brush the layers with coffee liqueur. Spread each layer with coffee buttercream, then cover the entire cake with the remaining cream.

8   Press toasted sliced almonds around the sides of the cake. Decorate the top with cocoa powder: place strips of paper diagonally across the cake in a lattice pattern, as illustrated; sift the cocoa powder over the surface and remove the paper strips.

Sachertorte

150 g/5 oz plain chocolate
1¹/₂ tbsp milk
6 eggs, separated
150 g/5 oz butter
250 g/9 oz sugar
100 g/3 oz ground almonds
125 g/4 oz flour
few drops vanilla essence
50 g/2 oz fine breadcrumbs
3 tbsp apricot jam
3 tbsp rum
chocolate icing*
butter to grease cake tin

1   Melt the chocolate over a low heat with the milk. Whisk the egg whites until stiff.

2   Cream the sugar with the butter, add the egg yolks, melted chocolate, almonds, whisked egg whites, flour, vanilla essence and breadcrumbs.

3   Pour the mixture into a buttered cake tin and place in a preheated oven at 200°C/400°F/mark 6 for 30 minutes. Remove and cool for several hours.

4   Cut the cake into three equal layers. Spread the first with apricot jam. Sprinkle the second layer with rum and place on top. Spread with apricot jam and cover with the third layer.

5   Cover the cake with chocolate icing. Leave smooth, or decorate with more finely piped icing.

Strawberry cream gâteau

1 20-cm/8-in sponge cake*
Grand Marnier or
   Maraschino to soak
400 g/14 oz strawberries
Chantilly cream*

1   Prepare the sponge.

2   When the cake has cooled cut it into three equal layers. Sprinkle each layer with the liqueur of your choice. Cut 150 g/5 oz strawberries in half.

3   Spread the first layer of sponge with Chantilly cream*; cover with halved strawberries.

4   Repeat with the second layer.

5   Cover with the third layer.

6   Cover the entire cake with Chantilly cream and decorate with cream rosettes, using a piping bag. Decorate the top and sides with the remaining strawberries.

Fruit cake

50 g/2 oz butter
80 g/3 oz icing sugar
$^{1}/_{2}$ tbsp clear honey
2 eggs
80 g/3 oz flour
1 tsp baking powder
175 g/6 oz sultanas
1 tbsp walnuts, coarsely
   chopped

2 tbsp rum
pinch cinnamon
pinch nutmeg
pinch allspice
1$^{1}/_{2}$ tbsp chopped candied
   peel
few glacé cherries
butter to grease tin

The fruit cake was an
English invention and is
justly famous all over the
world. The basic recipe can
be adapted to give a range
of variations: chopped
almonds and pistachios can
be added, or hazelnuts, or
Brazil nuts. Ginger cake is
another variation of the
same recipe which differs
from the other versions in
that it contains no nuts or
fruit but is flavoured with
ginger.

1   Cream the butter until light and smooth.

2   Stir in half the sugar a little at a time.

3   Stir in remaining sugar then add the honey.

4   Add the beaten eggs and mix well using a balloon whisk or electric beater.

5   Sift the flour with the baking powder and add to the mixture. Allow to rest.

6   Soak the sultanas and walnuts for about 30 minutes in a mixture of the rum, brandy, cinnamon, nutmeg and allspice. Stir these ingredients together with the candied peel and glacé cherries into the mixture from step 5.

7   Line a rectangular loaf tin with waxed paper buttered on both sides. Pour the mixture into the tin and smooth the surface with a spatula.

8   Bake in a preheated oven at 180°C/350°F/mark 4 for 1 hour or until cooked. The cake is cooked when a skewer inserted into the middle comes out clean.

Viennese ring

(Kugelhupf)

3 tbsp milk
125 g/4 oz plain flour
1 whole egg
1 7-g/¼-oz envelope active
   dry yeast
20 g/1 oz finely chopped
   candied peel
50 g/2 oz sultanas
1 tsp grated lemon peel
125 g/4 oz butter
3 egg yolks
almonds or hazelnuts,
   chopped
1 egg and 1 tsp icing sugar
butter to grease mould

1   In a bowl over simmering water work together the milk, flour, whole egg, yeast and chopped candied peel. Mix in the sultanas and grated lemon peel. Allow to rest over the hot water.

2   In a separate bowl mix the butter, icing sugar and egg yolks.

3   Combine the two mixtures.

4   Cover with a cloth and leave to rise over hot water. The dough should double in size.

5   Butter a kugelhupf mould (this has a central tube and high, fluted sides and can be used for savarins and other desserts). Press the chopped nuts to the sides of the tin. Place the dough in the tin and allow to stand for 30 minutes.

6   Bake in a preheated oven at 180°C/350°F/mark 4 for about 1 hour. Unmould while still hot and brush with the egg beaten with a little icing sugar. Before serving sprinkle with icing sugar.

Cream puffs

250 ml/9 fl oz water
125 g/4 oz butter
1 tbsp sugar
$^1/_2$ tsp salt
150 g/5 oz plain flour
few drops vanilla essence or
    1 tsp grated lemon peel
3-4 eggs
butter to grease and flour to
    dust baking tray
Chantilly cream* or pastry
    cream*

Choux pastry is used for
making profiteroles and
chocolate eclairs; it can also
be used for savoury dishes
(with salt, spices or cheese
added to the pastry instead
of sugar). The filling can be
mixed with chopped fresh or
candied fruit.

1 Put the water, butter, sugar and salt in a saucepan with high sides and bring to the boil over a moderate heat. Turn off the heat as soon as boiling point is reached.

2 Sift the flour into this mixture.

3 Over a moderate heat stir vigorously with a wooden spoon until the mixture thickens and begins to sizzle. Remove from the heat and allow to cool, stirring continuously.

4 Add the vanilla essence or the grated lemon peel. Add the eggs one by one, beating each egg a little first and adding it to the mixture gradually.

5 The paste should not be too soft; if it is, it means that the liquid was not reduced enough in step 3. To avoid too soft a mixture add the eggs one at a time, and do not add the fourth egg unless necessary.

6 Butter a baking tray and dust with flour.

7 Place the paste in little heaps on the baking tray, using a piping bag or a spoon. Bake in a preheated oven at 200°C/400°F/mark 6 for about 20 minutes. Allow to cool.

8 Prepare the Chantilly cream or the pastry cream and use a piping bag to fill the puffs with cream. Decorate with more cream, if desired.

Jam drops

150 g/5 oz butter
150 g/5 oz sugar
2 eggs
1 tsp grated lemon peel
2 tbsp Marsala
200 g/7 oz plain flour
4 tbsp apricot jam

1   Cream the butter in a bowl and stir in the sugar gradually. Add the eggs, lemon peel and Marsala and mix well. Sift the flour in gradually through a sieve, stirring until well blended. (If the dough is too firm add a few more teaspoons of Marsala.)

2   Allow to stand for an hour or two.

3   Use your hands to shape the dough into small balls about the size of walnuts. Place the dough balls on a buttered baking tray and flatten each one with the base of a glass to make "drops" 3 cm/1¹/₄ in in diameter. Make a well in the centre of each one with the end of a teaspoon and fill with 1 teaspoon jam.

4   Bake in a preheated oven at 180°C/350°F/mark 4 for 15 minutes.

Sponge fingers

150 g/5 oz sugar
6 egg yolks
150 g/5 oz plain flour
1 tsp salt
6 egg whites
25 g/1 oz icing sugar
50 g/2 oz caster sugar

1   Beat the sugar and egg yolks until creamy. Continuing to beat, gradually add the flour and salt.

2   Whisk the egg whites until they form stiff peaks. Fold carefully into the mixture, stirring from bottom to top until well mixed.

3   Using a piping bag with a wide plain nozzle, pipe the dough into strips 10 cm/4 in long on a well-buttered and floured baking tray.

4   Mix the two kinds of sugar and sprinkle over the fingers.

5   Bake in a preheated oven at 170°C/325°F/mark 3 for 15-20 minutes.

Brioche croissants

15 g/¹/₂ oz fresh yeast
3 tbsp milk
325 g/11 oz plain flour
2 tbsp sugar
1 tsp salt
1 whole egg
1 egg yolk
150 ml/5 fl oz milk
50 g/2 oz butter
80 g/3 oz softened butter
1 egg, beaten with 1 tbsp
  icing sugar
butter to grease and flour to
  dust

1   Mix the yeast with the milk and a few spoonfuls of flour.

2   Make a well in the centre of the remaining flour and mix in the sugar, salt, whole egg and yolk, milk and 50 g/2 oz butter.

3   Add the yeast mixture from step 1 and mix thoroughly.

4   Cover and leave to rise in a warm place until doubled in volume.

5   Roll out the dough with a rolling pin.

6   Spread the softened butter over a third of the dough with a spatula.

7   Fold the dough in three and roll out again. Place in the refrigerator for 15 minutes. Fold in three again and roll out with the rolling pin. Leave to rest in the refrigerator for another 15 minutes.

8   Roll out the dough to about 2 cm/³/₄ in thick and cut into triangles. Starting from the base roll up each triangle and curve into a crescent shape. Place on a buttered, floured baking tray and brush with egg beaten with a little icing sugar. Bake in a preheated oven at 230°C/450°F/mark 8 for 20 minutes.

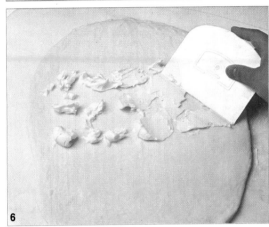

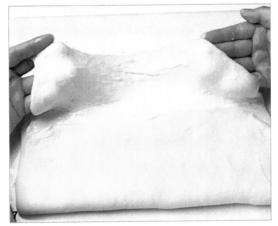

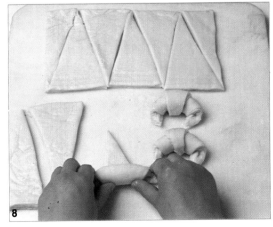

Rum babas

brioche dough (see page
  334)
butter to grease and flour to
  dust moulds

For the syrup:
225 ml/8 fl oz water
8 tbsp clear honey
6 tbsp rum

1   Prepare the dough using
the same ingredients and
quantities as for the brioches
described on page 334, but
bake the dough in baba
moulds.

2   To make the syrup:
simmer the water and honey
together for a few minutes.
Add the rum and simmer for
a few minutes more.

3   Soak the warm babas in
the rum syrup either by
pouring the syrup over them
or immersing them in the
syrup. Make small holes all
over the babas with a
skewer to allow the syrup to
penetrate. Serve
immediately.

Cream doughnuts

400 g/14 oz plain flour
250 ml/9 fl oz milk
20 g/³/₄ oz fresh yeast
80 g/3 oz butter
3 eggs
2 tbsp rum
4 tbsp sugar
¹/₂ tsp salt
few drops vanilla *essence*
Pastry cream*
icing sugar

1 Mix 50 g/2 oz flour with a little milk and the yeast. Roll the mixture into a ball and set it to rise in warm water until it floats and has doubled in size.

2 Melt the butter; add the eggs and rum. Stir in the remaining flour, sugar, salt and vanilla essence.

3 Add to the ball of yeast and mix well. If necessary add a little milk to make a soft, smooth dough. Set to rise until doubled in volume.

4 Knead the dough on a floured surface for about 15 minutes, until it no longer sticks to the fingers. Roll out to a thickness of ¹/₂-1 cm/¹/₄-¹/₂ in. Using a large glass cut circles from the pastry. Spinkle with flour and leave in a warm place to rise.

5 Deep fry in plenty of hot oil over a moderate heat until golden brown.

6 Drain and fill with pastry cream.

7 Sprinkle with icing sugar.

Scones

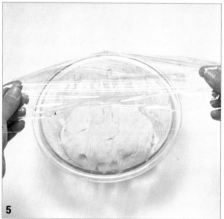

575 g/1¼ lb plain flour
1 tsp baking powder
½ tsp salt
1 tbsp grated orange or
   lemon peel
80 g/3 oz butter
4 tbsp sugar
2 eggs
220 ml/8 fl oz milk or single
   cream
1 beaten egg to glaze

1   Sift the flour together with the baking powder and salt into a bowl; add the grated orange peel.

2   Work in the softened butter.

3   Add the sugar and mix until well blended.

4   Add one egg and the milk or cream and knead lightly to make a soft dough.

5   Place the dough in a bowl and allow to rest for about 1 hour.

6   Roll out the dough to a thickness of about 2 cm/³⁄₄ in. Cut out the scones with a round pastry cutter. Transfer to a buttered baking tray. Brush the surface of the scones with the remaining beaten egg. Bake in a preheated oven at 200°C/400°F/mark 6 for 10-12 minutes.

Madeleines

melted butter to grease
80 g/3 oz butter
50 g/2 oz icing sugar
2 egg yolks
2 tbsp brandy
2 egg whites
50 g/2 oz plain flour
pinch salt
25 g/1 oz cornflour
few drops vanilla essence

This is a classic French
recipe from Alsace. The
traditional moulds are shell
shaped. Smaller moulds are
often used, the resulting
biscuits being called
madeleinettes. When
cooled, madeleines or
madeleinettes can be dusted
with icing sugar.

1   Brush the madeleine moulds with a little melted butter.

2   Melt 80 g/3 oz butter over hot water.

3   Sift the sugar to eliminate lumps.

4   In a bowl over simmering water mix together the sugar, egg yolks and brandy and stir until thick. Remove from the heat and transfer the mixture to another bowl to cool.

5   Beat the egg whites and blend in the flour and salt. Fold in mixture from step 4.

6   Add the cornflour and vanilla essence and mix well.

7   Add the melted butter from step 2 and mix well.

8   Pour the dough into the buttered moulds. Bake in a preheated oven at 200°C/400°F/mark 6 for about 10 minutes. Remove from the moulds at once and cool on a wire rack.

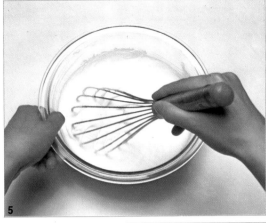

Meringues

3 egg whites
175 g/6 oz caster sugar

Meringue generally refers to a sweet made with stiffly beaten egg whites and sugar, cooked in a slow oven until firm. The basic recipe—50 g/2 oz sugar to each egg white—can be used to make various shapes, including rings, pyramids, pie toppings and nests. Meringue may also serve as a dessert base and can be filled with whipped cream, ice cream, custard or fruit. Flavour and colour can be changed by adding flavourings such as chocolate, coffee and vanilla. Flat meringues arranged in layers with sponge cake, buttercream, fruit and whipped cream, make an elegant and delicious party dessert.

1   Whisk the egg whites as stiffly as possible using a balloon whisk or electric beater.

2   Sift the sugar and fold in carefully so that the whites do not collapse.

3   Place the mixture in small heaps on a greased baking tray, using either a spoon or a piping bag with a large plain nozzle.

4   Bake immediately in a preheated oven at 110°C/225°F/mark ¼ until firm and dry.

Zuccotto

850 ml/1¹/₂ pints double cream
200 g/7 oz icing sugar
125 g/4 oz ground almonds
125 g/4 oz ground hazelnuts
2 tbsp candied peel
150 g/5 oz plain chocolate, grated
450 g/1 lb sponge cake*
2 tbsp brandy
2 tbsp rum
2 tbsp kirsch
1 tbsp Morello cherries
cocoa powder and icing sugar

1   In a deep bowl whip the cream and fold in the sugar carefully. Add the ground almonds, hazelnuts and candied peel. Divide the mixture between two bowls. Melt the chocolate, allow it to cool, then fold it into half the cream mixture.

2   Cut the sponge into slices 1-2 cm/¹/₂-³/₄ in thick and sprinkle with the three spirits mixed together. Line a mould or bowl with the slices.

3   Pour the plain cream mixture into the mould first. Place the Morello cherries in the centre. Pour the chocolate-flavoured cream into the mould.

4   Cover the cream with more sponge slices, not dipped in spirit.

5   Chill in the refrigerator for at least 2 hours.

6   Unmould the zuccotto on a serving dish. Decorate with cocoa powder and icing sugar.

Trifle with nuts

1 layer sponge cake*, about
   2.5 cm/1 in thick
sweet liqueur to soak
confectioner's custard*
Chantilly cream*
toasted nuts or caramelised
   dried fruit*

1   Place the sponge in a
glass dish approximately
23 cm/9 in in diameter.

2   Using a pastry brush,
brush the sponge with sweet
liqueur of your choice.

3   Spread the sponge with
a layer of confectioner's
custard 1 cm/$^1/_2$ in thick.

4   Decorate the cake with
toasted nuts or caramelised
dried fruit.

5   Place the cake in the
freezer for at least 30
minutes.

6   Before serving, decorate
the top of the cake with
Chantilly cream.

Trifle with meringue topping

600 g/1¹/₄ lb confectioner's
   custard*
275 g/10 oz sponge cake*
few drops red food
   colouring mixed with 3
   tbsp liqueur of choice
125 g/4 oz candied peel,
   diced
3 tbsp rum to soak sponge
5 egg whites
150 g/5 oz icing sugar
glacé cherries

1   Place 3 tablespoons of
the confectioner's custard in
a large, ovenproof glass dish
and place on top half the
sponge, cut into large
squares; sprinkle with the
liqueur mixture. Cover with
another layer of custard and
four fifths of the candied
peel.

2   Cover with a second
layer of sponge, sprinkled
with rum, and the remaining
custard.

3   Prepare the meringue
topping by whipping the egg
whites and carefully folding
in the icing sugar. Cover the
sponge with the meringue
and decorate with the
remaining candied peel, and
glacé cherries.

4   Place in a moderate
oven (180°C/350°F/mark 4)
for 3-5 minutes to brown the
meringue.

5   Serve well chilled.

Chocolate mousse

4 egg yolks
125 g/4 oz sugar
juice of 1 orange
125 g/4 oz plain chocolate
50 g/2 oz butter
2 tbsp Marsala or strong
  coffee
25 g/1 oz candied orange
  peel (optional)
3 egg whites
175 ml/6 fl oz whipping
  cream, lightly whipped

Chocolate mousse differs from all other types of mousse in that it does not contain the classic ingredients of a mousse—gelatine, cornflour or milk. When chocolate is melted and allowed to cool, it sets the mousse. No other setting agent is needed.

1   In a saucepan beat together the egg yolks and the sugar.

2   Place over a low heat, add the orange juice and stir until thickened.

3   Melt the chocolate with the butter and the Marsala or coffee in a bain-marie.

4   Stir the chocolate into the egg and orange mixture.

5   Add the candied orange peel.

6   Whisk the egg whites until firm.

7   Fold carefully into the chocolate until the mixture is well blended.

8   Pour into individual dishes or glasses and decorate with a layer of double or whipped cream. Place in the refrigerator until ready to serve.

Cherry liqueur bombe

Preparation: 30 minutes
(+ freezing time)

200 g/7 oz sugar
3 tbsp maraschino
3 egg yolks
400 g/14 oz tinned cherries
8 tbsp double cream

1   Mix together in a saucepan 100 g/3¹/₂ oz sugar and the maraschino (reserving 1 tablespoon); heat gently, stirring until bubbles form on the surface of the syrup. Remove from the heat and leave to cool.

2   Beat the egg yolks and 2 tablespoons sugar in a saucepan until creamy; place in a bain-marie over a low heat and whisk, gradually adding the liqueur syrup in a thin trickle. When frothy and warm, remove from the heat and leave to cool, stirring frequently.

3   Pour the cream into an ice-cream making machine and partially freeze.

4   Add one third of the finely chopped cherries to the cream and finish the freezing process. Divide between four individual moulds and place in the freezer for about 1 hour.

5   Meanwhile, blend the remaining fruit, reserving 4 cherries, with the double cream, a little sugar and 1 tablespoons maraschino. Chill in the refrigerator.

6   Unmould the individual fruit ice creams and pour the chilled cream on top. Decorate with the reserved cherries.

Ice cream

(Vanilla and coffee)

225 ml/8 fl oz milk
120 ml/4 fl oz double cream
few drops vanilla essence
3 egg yolks
50 g/2 oz icing sugar
1 tbsp coffee powder

1   For the vanilla ice cream boil the milk; for the coffee ice cream boil the milk and coffee. All the other stages and ingredients are the same for both ice creams.

2   Remove from the heat, cool slightly, add the cream and vanilla essence and cool for at least 15 minutes.

3   In a separate bowl beat together the egg yolks and sugar until pale and creamy.

4   Combine the egg yolks and sugar with the mixture from step 2, stirring constantly.

5   Place over a very low heat. Do not boil. Stir constantly until thick.

6   Remove from the heat, transfer to a clean bowl and stir until cool.

7   Pour into a shallow dish and keep in the freezer.

Mint sorbet, orange sorbet

For the mint sorbet:
125 g/4 oz sugar
125 ml/4 fl oz water
2 tbsp lemon juice
2 tbsp mint syrup
2 egg whites

For the orange sorbet:
125 g/4 oz sugar
275 ml/10 fl oz orange juice
2 tbsp kirsch or maraschino
2 egg whites

1   For the mint sorbet (steps 1-6): dissolve the sugar in the water over a low heat. Stir until boiling point is reached then remove from the heat.

2   Add the lemon juice and the mint syrup and stir.

3   Whisk the egg whites until stiff and fold into the mixture.

4   Place in a shallow container and freeze for 2 hours.

5   Remove and stir vigorously at intervals to avoid crystals forming as the sorbet freezes.

6   Replace in the freezer to harden and leave until ready to serve.

7   For the orange sorbet: dissolve the sugar in the orange juice over a low heat, stirring until thick. Remove from the heat and add the liqueur. Whisk the egg whites and fold in carefully. Place in a container in the freezer for 2 hours. Remove at intervals and beat until smooth. Replace in the freezer until ready to serve.

Yoghurt jelly

6 tsp icing sugar
1 150 g/5 oz carton yoghurt
2 tbsp sweet liqueur
60 ml/2 fl oz double cream
1 (7-g/¼-oz) envelope
  unflavoured powdered
  gelatine
3 tbsp water

1   Mix the sugar and the yoghurt. Add the liqueur and stir.

2   Whip the cream until stiff, then fold the cream carefully into the yoghurt.

3   Dissolve the gelatine in the hot water and add gradually to the yoghurt mixture.

4   Pour into moulds, and place in the refrigerator.

5   Turn out into individual glass dishes.

6   Decorate with slices of lime and fresh mint leaves.

Cointreau jellies with orange sauce

1 (7-g/¼-oz) envelope
  unflavoured powdered
  gelatine
3 tbsp hot water
50 g/2 oz sugar
2 egg yolks
300 ml/½ pint milk
2 tbsp Cointreau
2 egg whites

1   Put the gelatine and the hot water in a bowl to soften the gelatine.

2   Beat together the sugar and egg yolks until creamy. Add the milk and mix.

3   Add the gelatine and the liqueur.

4   Keep the mixture warm over a bowl of hot water until needed.

5   Beat the egg whites until stiff.

6   Fold carefully into the cream, stirring carefully from bottom to top.

7   Pour into moulds and allow to set.

8   Prepare the orange sauce: dissolve the sugar in the orange juice over a low heat. Bring to the boil, then remove from the heat. Allow to cool. To serve, turn out the individual moulds on to a serving dish and pour round the orange sauce.

Basic Recipes

The following section lists, in alphabetical order, ingredients, utensils and preparation instructions referred to in the book.

AÏOLI

4 cloves garlic
2 egg yolks
salt and pepper
250 ml/9 fl oz olive oil
1 lemon

Peel the garlic and crush in a mortar. Stir together the egg yolks, garlic, salt and pepper. Pour in the oil a drop at a time, stirring constantly. Add the lemon juice in the same way and continue stirring until smooth.

ALMOND PASTE

450 g/1 lb almonds
450 g/1 lb caster sugar
3 tbsp corn syrup or golden syrup
175 ml/6 fl oz water
icing sugar, if needed

Preheat oven to 180°C/350°/mark 4. Soak almonds in boiling water 5 to 10 minutes or until skins loosen and can be peeled off easily. Peel almonds; place on a baking tray. Place in oven to dry and toast. Toast only until lightly coloured, about 3-5 minutes. If allowed to burn, almonds cannot be used for almond paste. Grind toasted almonds in batches in a blender or food processor to make a fine flour. Lightly oil a marble slab or baking tray. In a medium saucepan, dissolve caster sugar and syrup in water. Boil until mixture reaches the soft-ball stage (115°C/238°F). While still hot, blend sugar syrup with ground almonds. Pour mixture onto oiled marble or baking tray. Work with a spatula until mixture is cool enough to handle. Then knead until smooth, dusting with powdered sugar as needed. For immediate use, let paste stand at least 2 hours. Store tightly covered in a cool place. If paste becomes too hard to shape easily, wrap in foil and steam over boiling water until softened. Almond paste can be coloured or flavoured with liqueurs or essences. Makes about 900 g/2 lb.

BAIN-MARIE & DOUBLE BOILER

The term bain-marie describes a method of cooking liquid or solid foods in a container placed in boiling water. To make a bain-marie, place a saucepan, small baking or soufflé dish or ramekins in a baking tin half-full of water. The outer pan should be no more than half-full so no water splashes into the food.
A double boiler is two pans fitted one inside the other. The bottom pan holds water that does not touch the top pan.
Both methods are generally used for cooking sauces, custards and egg dishes, and when melting chocolate. It prevents them from overheating or curdling and keeps them hot. The temperature of the food never reaches boiling point.

BAKING

Oven temperatures are as follows:
Cool	130 to 150°C/250 to 300°F/mark	1/2-2
Warm	150 to 170°C/300 to 325°F/mark	2-3
Moderate	170 to 200°C/325 to 400°F/mark	3-6
Hot	200 to 230°C/400 to 450°F/mark	6-8

Always preheat the oven before baking cakes, biscuits, soufflés, sweet breads and other desserts unless the recipe dictates otherwise. Plan your recipe preparation and preheating of the oven so food doesn't have to wait for the oven to heat.
During baking, keep the oven door closed. Opening the door will cause the temperature to drop. Cakes and soufflés, in particular, might be ruined. If it is absolutely unavoidable or if the recipe instructs you to do so, carefully open the door, avoiding a sudden draft of air. Close it as quickly as possible.

BÉARNAISE SAUCE

Makes approximately 4 servings
2 shallots
125 ml/4 fl oz white wine
75 ml/3 fl oz vinegar
1 1/2 tbsp chopped tarragon
1 1/2 tbsp chopped chervil
3 egg yolks
250 g/9 oz butter
salt
pinch Cayenne pepper

Finely chop the shallots and place in a saucepan with the wine, vinegar and 1 tablespoon each tarragon and chervil. Reduce over a low heat for about 15 minutes until approximately 3 tablespoons of liquid remain. Strain through a chinois, pressing well to extract as much liquid as possible. Pour into a double saucepan or into a small basin over a saucepan of simmering water. Mix in the egg yolks, beating with a whisk. Gradually add the softened butter, beating carefully and making sure that each piece is well blended before adding the next. Remove from the heat and continue beating. The sauce should be quite thick. Add the remaining tarragon and chervil and season with salt and Cayenne pepper. Mix well.

BEEF CONSOMMÉ

1.5 litres/2 1/2 pints homemade meat stock, all fat removed
225 g/1/2 lb stewing beef
1 onion
1 clove garlic
1 carrot
1 celery stalk
pinch of thyme
3 peppercorns
1 egg white
salt

Trim off any fat from the beef; mince or chop finely and place in a large pot or saucepan. Scrub the carrot, peel the onion and chop them with the celery and garlic and add to the beef. Add a pinch of salt, the thyme, the egg white and the black peppercorns and mix well. Pour in the cold beef stock and bring to the boil, stirring constantly. Turn down the heat, cover and simmer for 1 hour. Strain the consommé through a fine sieve lined with a piece of muslin before serving.

BEEF CONSOMMÉ WITH SHERRY

Follow the recipe above, stirring in 4 tablespoons medium dry sherry at the end of the cooking time, before straining.

BEURRE BLANC

1 shallot, chopped
1 1/2 tbsp white wine vinegar
1 tbsp white wine
1 tbsp fumet (q.v.)
125 g/4 oz butter
salt and pepper

Place the shallot, vinegar, wine and fumet in a saucepan and cook over a moderate heat until the liquid has reduced by three quarters. Remove from the heat. Leave to cool slightly before beating in the butter as quickly as possible, one piece at a time. Make sure the butter is well blended and the sauce pale and creamy. Season with salt and pepper. (If the sauce turns transparent, plunge the bottom of the saucepan into iced water until the sauce thickens.)

BISCUITS

Biscuits are usually sweet and are made with liquid, flour, butter, sugar, eggs and flavourings. They are quite easy to make. Use fresh ingredients, and be sure to measure them carefully. Use baking trays with very low or no edges. Baking tins with high sides prevent biscuits from browning evenly. Bake biscuits in the centre of the oven if only one baking tray is being used. If two baking trays are being used at the same time, leave space between them for air to circulate. Cut biscuits the same size to ensure even cooking.

Types of biscuits:

Bars
Biscuits are baked in one piece, then cut into slices or squares when cooled.

Dropped
Biscuits are made with dough that is too soft to be rolled with a rolling pin. The dough is spooned on to the baking tray.

Rolled
Biscuits are flattened with a rolling pin, then cut out with fancy cutters or shaped by hand.

Piped
The dough is piped through a piping bag, according to the shape desired.

Refrigerator dough is usually rolled into a cylinder and stored in the refrigerator or freezer. When firm, it is sliced or shaped into thin biscuits.
Some biscuits are sandwiched together with cream cheese, jam, flavoured creams or fruit fillings. Tops of biscuits may be decorated with chocolate or glacé icing, nuts, candied peel, jam, caster or icing sugar, coconut or other decorative items.
Biscuits keep best in an airtight container or in the freezer wrapped in foil. Never put crisp and soft, moist biscuits together in the same container. The moisture from the moist biscuits will soften crisp biscuits.

BUTTERCREAM

200 g/7 oz butter or margarine
125 g/4 oz icing sugar
4 egg yolks
2 egg whites, if a lighter cream is desired

In a medium bowl, cream butter or margarine and sugar until light and fluffy. Beat in egg yolks, one at a time. Whisk egg whites until stiff but not dry. Gently fold beaten egg whites into butter mixture. Makes about 350 g/12 oz.

Variations:

Vanilla buttercream
Beat in 1 teaspoon vanilla essence with egg yolks.

Liqueur buttercream
Beat in 1½ tablespoons liqueur of choice with egg yolks.

Hazelnut buttercream
After folding in beaten egg whites, fold in 50 g/2 oz ground toasted hazelnuts.

Pistachio or almond buttercream
After folding in beaten egg whites, fold in 30-50 g/1-2 oz finely chopped or ground pistachios or almonds.

Lemon buttercream
Beat in 1½ tablespoons lemon juice with egg yolks.

Chocolate buttercream
Beat in 50 g/2 oz melted cooking chocolate with egg yolks.

Coffee buttercream
Beat in 2 teaspoons instant coffee powder with egg yolks.

Pistachio Grand Marnier buttercream
Beat in 1½ tablespoons Grand Marnier with egg yolks. After folding in beaten egg whites, fold in 25 g/1 oz finely chopped or ground pistachios.

CAPER SAUCE

2 tbsp capers
1 clove garlic
1 tbsp anchovy paste
250 ml/9 fl oz olive oil
juice of ½ lemon

Pound the capers and garlic or blend in a food processor. Place in a bowl and mix in the anchovy paste. Stir in the olive oil gradually, followed by the lemon juice and mix until well blended.

CARAMELISED FRUIT

150 g/5 oz sugar
5 tbsp water
fruit of your choice

In a small saucepan, cook sugar and water until light brown. Dip fruit in caramelised sugar. Allow the sugar to harden, then dip the fruit in caramelised sugar again. Makes about 100 ml/4 fl oz.

Both fresh and dried fruit can be caramelised by following this method. Crystallised and citrus peel can also be caramelised. These can be sandwiched together with a marzipan filling (q.v.) before being caramelised.

CHANTILLY CREAM

350 ml/12 fl oz whipping cream
25 g/1 oz icing sugar

In a large bowl, whip cream until soft peaks form. Beat in sugar to taste until stiff peaks form.

Chantilly cream is sweetened whipped cream. Unsweetened whipped cream and whipped cream with sugar and vanilla essence added are sometimes incorrectly called Chantilly cream. In spite of extensive research, no one knows where or when the name originated.

CHICKEN STOCK

bones and carcass of 1 chicken
½ leek
1 onion, halved
2 carrots
1 bouquet garni
12 peppercorns
salt
1 bay leaf

Place all the ingredients in a large saucepan or stockpot. Cover with cold water and bring to the boil. Skim, cover and simmer for 3 hours. Strain and allow the stock to cool. When cold, remove the solid white fat, strain again and store in the refrigerator or freezer.

CHOCOLATE ICING

175 ml/6 fl oz whipping cream

200 g/7 oz plain chocolate
50 g/2 oz icing sugar
1 tsp vanilla essence

Combine the cream and 150 g/5 oz chocolate. Cook over a medium heat until chocolate melts and mixture begins to boil. Stir well. Refrigerate until slightly warm. Beat until smooth. Beat in icing sugar and vanilla essence.

CLARIFIED BUTTER

450 g/1 lb butter

Melt the butter in a saucepan over a moderate heat and simmer for 5 minutes. Remove any surface scum with a slotted spoon, then pour the clarified butter into a clean bowl, making sure the residue which collects in the bottom of the saucepan is left behind.

COCOA & CHOCOLATE

Cocoa powder is extracted from fruit seeds of the cocoa plant grown in tropical regions of the world. Each cocoa fruit is 20-25-cm/8-10-in long and contains as many as 60 seeds.
The process of extracting cocoa is complicated. Seeds are allowed to ferment in the open air or underground. Then they are washed, dried, roasted and fermented a second time. They are again washed and dried, then they are ground. At this time, cocoa butter is separated from the seeds. Cocoa seeds contain a large quantity of oil and fat that is used in the manufacture of cosmetics, medicines and chocolate.
The major use of cocoa is for the manufacture of chocolate, but it is widely used in pastries, confectionery and in milk drinks.
Chocolate is manufactured by heating cocoa powder with a good portion of cocoa butter. It is then allowed to set in various shapes and thicknesses. To melt chocolate, grate or break block chocolate into small pieces. Place in top of a double boiler or in a saucepan over or in a pan of simmering water. If the melting chocolate remains thick or develops lumps, add a little margarine – never butter – and reduce the heat. Unused chocolate can be saved, but must be melted again.

CONFECTIONER'S CUSTARD

430 ml/¾ pint milk
120 ml/4 fl oz single cream
1 tsp grated lemon peel or orange peel, or 1 tsp vanilla essence
175 g/6 oz sugar
1 tsp cornflour
10 egg yolks, beaten

Reserve 5 tablespoons milk. In a medium saucepan, combine remaining milk and cream. Place over a low heat. Add lemon or orange peel or vanilla. Gradually add sugar, stirring constantly. Blend reserved milk with cornflour. Add to hot milk mixture. Stirring constantly, bring to the boil. Remove from heat. Add 225 ml/8 fl oz hot milk mixture slowly to beaten egg yolks. Then add egg-yolk mixture to remaining hot milk mixture, stirring constantly. Return to heat until custard thickens. Do not overcook. This can be done in a double boiler to prevent overcooking. Makes about 750 ml/1¼ pints.

COURT-BOUILLON

1 carrot
5 peppercorns
2 litres/3½ pints water
6 tbsp white wine
3 tbsp white wine vinegar
½ tbsp sea salt
½ celery stalk
2 sprigs parsley
½ onion
½ bay leaf
pinch thyme

Cut the carrot into four lengthwise, crush the peppercorns, and place all the ingredients in a large saucepan. Bring to the boil, simmer for 30 minutes, then strain through a sieve. This rich *court-bouillon* is ideal for fish such as turbot and eel. For a simpler version, reduce the quantity of vegetables and use half the quantity of wine and vinegar. This quantity will be sufficient for 1 kg/2¼ lb fish.

CREAM CUSTARD

350 ml/12 fl oz milk
50 g/2 oz icing sugar
1 tbsp plain flour
1 tbsp cornflour
2 egg yolks, beaten
15 g/½ oz butter

In a medium saucepan, scald 225 ml/8 fl oz milk. In a medium bowl, combine remaining milk, sugar, flour and cornflour, stir to blend. Add mixture to scalded milk. Simmer, stirring constantly, until thickened. Add ½ to ¾ of hot mixture to beaten egg yolks; then add egg-yolk mixture to remaining milk mixture, stirring constantly. Add butter, beating well. Return to heat until mixture simmers. Cool. Makes about 450 ml/¾ pint.

CREAMED PEPPER SAUCE

2 sweet red or yellow peppers
120 ml/4 fl oz single cream
salt

Place the sweet peppers in a hot oven, 200°C/400°F/mark 6, or under the grill until the skins blister and can be rubbed off. Skin the peppers and discard the seeds. Cut into small pieces and place in a blender or food processor with the cream and a pinch of salt. Blend until smooth; transfer to a small saucepan or frying pan, cover and simmer for

5 minutes, stirring with a whisk. Serve with pasta.

DEEP FRYING

When deep frying, use a pan with high sides so the oil will not overflow when food is being cooked.
Recipes often call for moderately hot, hot and very hot fat. These are as follows:

Moderately hot fat
Uses a low, steady heat to cook food inside before the outside becomes too crisp or begins to burn.

Hot fat
Has a constant, moderate heat underneath. It is used for sweets that are already partly cooked then coated in batter. The outside is cooked until crisp and golden without overcooking the inside.

Very hot fat
Uses high heat to cook small pieces of food that must cook rapidly without burning. After frying one batch of food, let the oil become hot again before adding more food. If the oil is not hot enough, it soaks into the food, making it soggy and preventing a crisp, golden crust.
If you do not have a deep-fat thermometer, use the bread-cube method to determine temperatures. When deep frying, a 2.5-cm/1-in cube of bread will turn golden brown at these temperatures and times:

178-183°C/345-355°F	65 seconds
184-187°C/356-365°F	60 seconds
188-191°C/366-375°F	50 seconds
192-195°C/376-385°F	40 seconds
195-198°C/386-395°F	20 seconds

FISH

Choosing fish

For serious cooks and lovers of fish, truly fresh fish can only be considered that which, as soon as it is caught, is sorted into shallow boxes on a bed of ice and transported immediately to a quayside market. When buying fish it is essential to know how to judge its freshness from its appearance, texture and smell.
Freshly caught fish is quite stiff, although this characteristic changes after only a few hours; the skin is taut, bright, and shiny; the scales lie flat against the body, which is covered with a thin, translucent film. The pupil should be dark and bright and the cornea shining and transparent. The flesh beneath the gill flap should be bright red and the fish should be firm and resistant to the touch; the flesh should spring back when pressed lightly.
As for judging the freshness of fish by its smell, a few simple comparisons may help: fresh fish should smell of the sea and of the strong but pleasant saltiness of seaweed. When checking

the freshness of molluscs and crustaceans the appearance of the body is the most important indicator; crustaceans should be shiny, wet, and firm, vividly coloured with their legs or claws firmly attached to their bodies. They should smell fresh and of the sea. The colour of the body of molluscs may vary, depending on their colour when caught, as they often camouflage themselves. The whiteness of the flesh of cuttlefish and squid is a sign of freshness; yellow or brownish patches show that they are not fresh. The state of the shells is a good indication of the freshness of mussels, clams, or oysters. They should be tightly closed or should snap shut when sharply tapped if the molluscs are still alive. As with fish, they should smell pleasantly salty and fresh.

Cooking fish

Fish lends itself to a variety of cooking methods, depending on the quality and texture of the flesh: it can be poached, cooked in foil (*en papillote*), shallow-fried, deep-fried, baked, grilled, barbecued, braised or steamed.

Poaching
The fish is cooked by simmering in a rich vegetable *court-bouillon* (*q.v.*) or lighter stock, depending on the type of fish. The stock should be allowed to cool before use and should always be kept below boiling point while the fish is cooking.

Cooking in foil
Fish cooked *en papillote* is placed together with the herbs and seasonings in the centre of a well-buttered sheet of foil. The edges are folded tightly to seal, forming a loose parcel, and the fish is baked in the oven or cooked in a steamer.

Shallow frying
Suitable for fillets and steaks. The fish is usually floured then fried in melted butter or oil.

Deep frying
Suitable for whole fish or fillets coated in batter. The fish is cooked in hot oil (180-190°C/350-370°F) and should be well drained on kitchen paper to absorb excess fat before serving.

Baking
All the ingredients, including the fish, are placed in an ovenproof dish or casserole and baked in the oven.

Grilling or barbecuing
The most important points to remember when cooking fish this way are the evenness of temperature and the distance of the fish from the source of heat. The fish should be slowly and evenly cooked. To prepare the fish, either soak in brine or brush with oil. Brush several times during cooking.

Braising
In this method the fish is browned lightly first in a little melted butter and then cooked either

in the oven or on top of the stove in wine, stock, tomato sauce or other liquid.

Steaming
The fish is cooked, with herbs and seasonings, on a plate or wrapped in foil and placed in a perforated metal basket or steamer over a saucepan of simmering water.

Storing fish
To keep fish for a short period – not more than 24 hours – clean in the usual way, wrap in clingfilm, and place in the refrigerator. To keep fish for longer than a day it should be stored in the freezer. Rinse and clean the fish thoroughly, dry with kitchen paper, and cut into fillets or steaks. Frozen fish, which, strictly speaking, should have been brought from room temperature to 0°C/32°F in less than 4 hours, should be stored at that temperature until it is used. Frozen fish is usually packaged in plastic bags so that you can check the state of the fish. Once removed from the freezer it must be used without delay. Always pay careful attention to the recommended storage dates on frozen fish.

FISH ASPIC

1 onion
1 carrot
1 celery stalk
oil
bouquet garni
350 g/³/₄ lb fish trimmings (heads, bones, etc.)
water
150 g/5 oz filleted white fish
1 egg
2 tbsp dry white wine
1 envelope powdered gelatine (optional)

Sauté an onion, a carrot and a celery stalk in a little oil in a large saucepan together with a bouquet garni. When the vegetables have softened, add the fish trimmings and water and bring to the boil. Simmer, covered, for 30 minutes. Remove from the heat and strain through a fine sieve. To clarify the liquid, allow to cool completely and then add the white filleted fish, and the white of an egg and the shell, finely crushed. Beat well with a balloon whisk and heat gently for 10-15 minutes. When the liquid is tepid, add the dry white wine and stir. Strain through a muslin cloth. In order to ensure that the fish aspic sets more rapidly and reliably, you can add an envelope of gelatine, dissolved in the fish aspic over a gentle heat.

FISH FUMET

1.4 litres/2¹/₂ pints of water
225 ml/8 fl oz dry white wine
700 g/1¹/₂ lb fish trimmings (heads, bones, etc.)
1 onion
1 celery stalk
1 carrot
1 bay leaf
black peppercorns

Bring the water and wine to the boil in a large saucepan. Add the fish trimmings, sliced onion, the celery stalk, carrot, bay leaf and a few black peppercorns. Simmer gently over a moderate heat for 40 minutes; leave to cool and then strain through a fine sieve.

FISH STOCK

225 g/¹/₂ lb fish trimmings (heads, bones, etc.)
450 g/1 lb assorted fish
1.8 litres/3 pints water
225 ml/8 fl oz dry white wine
1 celery stalk
1 leek
1 onion
1 bay leaf
pinch of thyme
salt

Coarsely chop the fish trimmings and place in a large saucepan with 450 g/1 lb assorted fish. Pour in the water and dry white wine. Bring slowly to boiling point. Add the coarsely chopped celery, the leek and the peeled and quartered onion, a bay leaf, a pinch of thyme and a little salt. Simmer gently for 40 minutes. Strain.

FRANGIPANE CREAM

2 egg yolks
125 g/4 oz sugar
25 g/1 oz plain flour
25 g/1 oz finely ground almonds
450 ml/³/₄ pint milk
vanilla essence

In a large bowl, beat egg yolks and sugar until pale and creamy. Beat in flour and ground almonds. Gradually stir in milk and vanilla. Place a fine sieve over a medium saucepan. Pour mixture through sieve to remove any lumps. Stir constantly over a low heat until thick and smooth. Makes about 700 ml/1 pint.

GLAZES

Honey glaze
Melt honey over a low heat with a few spoonfuls of water.

Honey glaze with liqueur
To the above add a few drops of liqueur. Stir until blended and slightly reduced. The spirit most often used is rum. White rum gives a pale glaze while dark rum results in a dark glaze.

Jam glaze
Melt a few tablespoons of jam over a low heat. The jam will become more liquid and will be easy to brush while still warm. For a thinner glaze, dilute jam with a little water. The jams most frequently used in baking are apricot, which gives a golden glaze, and raspberry,

which gives a reddish glaze. Fruit jelly can also be used as a glaze in the same way.

Rum glaze
Melt icing sugar with a little rum in a saucepan over a low heat. Stir to blend. Use 1 to 2 tablespoons rum per 125 g/4 oz icing sugar.

HOLLANDAISE SAUCE

2 large egg yolks
1 tbsp white wine vinegar
salt and pepper
225 g/8 oz butter
1 tbsp lemon juice

Beat together in a small bowl or double boiler the egg yolks, vinegar, salt and pepper. Heat very gently over a saucepan of gently simmering water, stirring constantly and adding the butter one piece at a time. Make sure each piece is well blended before adding the next. When all the butter is added and the sauce coats the back of a spoon, remove from the heat and stir in the lemon juice. Mix well and serve hot.

HSAO MAI DUMPLING CASES

225 g/8 oz strong flour
pinch salt

Makes 36

Sift the flour into a bowl; form a well in the centre and add 200 ml/7 fl oz boiling water, stirring quickly until a smooth, fairly thick dough is obtained. Knead the dough for 3 minutes and then roll into a long, cylindrical sausage shape.
Cut the roll into 36 portions and roll each portion into a ball. Flour the pastry board lightly and, using a lightly floured rolling pin, roll each ball out into a circle about 7 cm/2³/₄ in in diameter.
The dough sheets can be kept in the refrigerator if made in advance.

ICE CREAM, SORBET & SHERBET

Basic ingredients of ice cream are sugar, milk or cream, eggs and flavouring, such as vanilla, chocolate, lemon or strawberry. Ice cream is made by blending the ingredients as they freeze or freezing the blended ingredients, then beating to make them smooth and creamy.
Sorbets are frozen combinations of fruit purées, such as pineapple, orange and strawberry, blended with sugar syrup or another sweetener. Gelatine or whipped egg white are sometimes added to give them a light, fluffy texture.
Sherbets are made from fruit purée, juice and sweeteners or may contain wine or liqueur.

They contain no milk or eggs, and must be stirred during freezing to reduce the ice crystals. Or the frozen mixture can be scraped to resemble finely crushed ice.

ICING

Icing is used to cover cakes, breads and rolls. Use a soft icing on breads and rolls so it can be drizzled. When the icing is spread, it must be soft enough to spread easily before it hardens. Cake icing should be thick so it does not drip. A very thin icing can be used as a glaze. Spread it over the cake. Let it dry before adding the thicker icing. This keeps crumbs from mixing with the icing. Fruit-based jellies can also be used as glazes.

Chocolate icing
See page 357.

Fondant icing
325 g/11 oz sugar
$^1/_2$ teaspoon cream of tartar
175 ml/6 fl oz water

In a large, heavy saucepan, combine sugar and cream of tartar. Stir in water. Stir over low heat until sugar dissolves. Cover and bring to the boil. Remove cover; boil until mixture reaches soft-ball stage (115°C/238°F). Cool to room temperature. Beat vigorously with a wooden spoon until white and creamy. Use immediately to ice a cake. If fondant becomes too stiff to spread, add a little hot water, then beat until smooth.

Glacé icing
225 g/8 oz icing sugar
3 tbsp hot water

Sieve sugar into a large bowl. Icing sugar should always be sieved before making icing. Stir in water, a little at a time, until mixture forms a thick, smooth paste of coating consistency.

Variations
Add any of the following flavourings: cocoa powder, chocolate, coffee, Grand Marnier or other liqueurs, orange, lemon, caramel, cream cheese, strawberry, cherry, milk, fruit juice, almond essence, rose water or vanilla essence. Icing can also be tinted any desired colour.

Weeping icing
Add more water so mixture is thinner. This is often used on babas.

Royal icing
In place of water, use 1 egg white for each 175 g/6 oz icing sugar. Lightly beat egg white. Sift sugar as it is gradually stirred into egg white. Add a few drops of lemon juice to make icing whiter. Icing is ready when it will stand up in peaks. Store in a glass container. To use again, heat gently; add a few drops of water, if necessary.

LEAVENING AGENTS

Yeast
When combined with flour, moisture and warmth, yeast begins to ferment and converts flour into alcohol and carbon dioxide. These gas bubbles are what leavens bread. Oven heat kills the yeast and causes the gas to expand, raising the bread in a final *oven spring.*
Active dried yeast comes in 7 g/$^1/_4$ oz envelopes or in bulk. *Compressed fresh yeast* comes in cakes. Four level teaspoons or 15 g/$^1/_2$ oz of dried yeast is the equivalent of 25 g/1 oz of fresh yeast.
Active dried yeast has been dehydrated. The cells become active when mixed with a warm liquid. Store dried yeast in a cool, dry place – not in the refrigerator or freezer. Use by the expiry date on the packet. Or, *proof the yeast* by combining 1 envelope active dried yeast or 1 cake compressed fresh yeast, 1 teaspoon sugar and 3 tablespoons warm water. If the yeast begins to bubble and swell, it is active. If not, discard the yeast and begin with another packet.
Compressed fresh yeast must be refrigerated and used within 1 to 2 weeks or by the expiry date on the packet. It should always be proofed.

Baking soda or bicarbonate of soda
This reacts when moistened. It is especially volatile when combined with an acid liquid, such as buttermilk. It immediately gives off carbon dioxide. Always blend it with other dry ingredients before it is moistened, then bake as soon as possible.

Baking powder
This is a combination of baking soda and cream of tartar. *Single-acting* baking powder immediately releases its gas into the batter. *Double-acting* baking powder releases some gas when it is moistened and again when the batter is heated.
To ensure even distribution of baking soda or baking powder and even rising of the dough, blend with other dry ingredients before adding liquid.
Too much baking soda or baking powder gives a baked product a dry, crumbly texture and a bitter taste. It also causes the product to overrise and fall. Too little baking soda or baking powder makes a product heavy and gummy.

LEMON MARINADE

2-3 lemons

Lemons are used as a marinade for raw fish. Clean, rinse and dry the fish and leave to stand in the lemon juice for 30 minutes to 1 hour, depending on the size of the fish. Do not leave for too long as the acid will make the flesh flaccid.

MARZIPAN

450 g/1 lb caster sugar
150 ml/5 fl oz water
pinch of cream of tartar
350 g/12 oz finely ground, blanched almonds
2 egg whites, beaten stiff but not dry
80 g/3 oz icing sugar

Lighly oil a marble slab or baking tray. Dissolve caster sugar in water over a medium heat. Add cream of tartar; stir until dissolved. Boil without stirring until mixture reaches the soft-ball stage (115°C/238°F). Remove from heat. Stir in almonds and beaten egg whites. Return to heat 2 to 3 minutes, stirring constantly. Turn onto oiled marble or baking tray. Work paste with a spatula 5 to 10 minutes, bringing edges to centre. When cool enough to work by hand, knead until smooth. Use icing sugar, if necessary, to keep paste from sticking. Makes about 900 g/2 lb. Marzipan can be used to decorate large cakes or it can be made into small marzipan cakes. It can be shaped and coloured in a variety of ways, and is often moulded into fruit-shapes that can be glazed and coloured. Marzipan and almond paste (*q.v.*) are similar, and are often confused. Almond paste is used mainly as a filling for cakes and biscuits. Marzipan is used mainly for decoration.

MAYONNAISE

2 eggs
salt
200 ml/7 fl oz best quality olive oil
juice of $^1/_4$ lemon

Separate two eggs and beat the yolks lightly with a fork, seasoning with a little salt. Add to the yolks 200 ml/7 fl oz of very good quality olive oil a few drops at a time, beating with a wooden spoon until the mayonnaise thickens. Carefully beat in the juice of quarter of a lemon, adding a few drops at a time. This basic mayonnaise, perhaps the most famous of all cold sauces, can be flavoured in many different ways for a wide variety of dishes.

Green mayonnaise
Mayonnaise made with 2 egg yolks (see recipe above)
50 g/2 oz spinach
a few basil leaves
small bunch parsley
salt and pepper

Wash the spinach leaves thoroughly in cold running water to remove all traces of grit. Cook briefly in a covered saucepan with no added water. Drain when tender and chop finely. Chop the basil and parsley and mix with the spinach. Work into the mayonnaise and season with salt and pepper.

MEAT ASPIC

2 pieces of shin of beef
2 calf's feet

100 g/3½ oz pork rind
1 onion
1 celery stalk
1 carrot
bouquet garni (parsley, thyme, bay leaf)
salt
2 litres/3 pints water
2 eggs

Place all the ingredients, with the exception of the egg whites and shells, in a large saucepan. Bring to the boil over a high heat. Turn down the heat and simmer very gently for 2-3 hours, or until the liquid has reduced to half its original volume. Skim off any scum that rises to the top. Strain the stock through a fine sieve. Leave to cool then clarify by adding the whites and crushed shells of two eggs; return to a clean saucepan and heat gently over a low heat, stirring with a balloon whisk. When the stock reaches boiling point simmer for 10 minutes. Turn off the heat and leave to cool for 10 minutes before straining through a damp muslin cloth.

MEAT SAUCE

15 g/½ oz butter
275 g/10 oz minced beef
50 g/2 oz fresh spicy sausage
1 bay leaf
½ onion
1 clove
salt
225 g/8 oz tomatoes

Melt the butter in a heavy saucepan; add the minced beef, crumbled sausage, bay leaf and the ½ onion stuck with a clove, and cook over a low heat for 20 minutes, stirring frequently. Add salt and the skinned, seeded and chopped tomatoes; bring to the boil and simmer for about 1 hour, adding a little stock or warm water and 1 teaspoon meat extract if the sauce becomes too dry. Cook for a further 20 minutes then remove the onion and bay leaf.

MOCK MEAT SAUCE

1 onion
1 celery stalk
1 carrot
1 tbsp olive oil
50 g/2 oz fatty ham
250 ml/9 fl oz white wine
350 g/12 oz tomatoes
salt and pepper
1 tbsp chopped fresh parsley and marjoram

Mince the onion, celery and carrot. Heat the olive oil in a frying pan and brown the chopped vegetables and finely sliced ham. Add the wine, heat for 2 minutes then add the chopped tomatoes. Season with salt and pepper and cook over a medium heat for about 45 minutes.

MORNAY SAUCE

100 g/3½ oz butter

25 g/1 oz flour
250 ml/9 fl oz milk
salt
125 g/4 oz grated Parmesan

Make a white sauce: melt 40 g/1½ oz butter in a small saucepan, add the flour and stir over heat for 1 minute. Gradually stir in the hot milk, waiting for the sauce to thicken after each addition. Add salt to taste, then simmer for about 10 minutes. Add the remaining butter, cut into pieces, and the grated Parmesan and mix well. This sauce goes very well with fish.

NANTUA SAUCE

225 g/8 oz freshwater crayfish
salt
150 g/5 oz butter
25 g/1 oz flour
250 ml/9 fl oz milk
250 ml/9 fl oz fumet (q.v.)
pepper
150 ml/5 fl oz double cream

Boil the crayfish whole in salted water for 8 minutes without peeling; chop into pieces while still hot. Place in a blender or food processor with 125 g/4 oz melted butter and liquidize. Strain through a fine sieve. Make a white sauce: melt the remaining butter in a saucepan. Stir in the flour and cook gently for 2 minutes. Remove from the heat and stir in a little hot milk. Beat until smooth. Return to the heat and add the remaining milk and fumet. Season with salt and pepper. Bring to the boil, then simmer for 3 minutes. Add the cream and reduce slightly. Remove from the heat and stir in the crayfish butter.

NUTS, GRINDING & TOASTING

Almonds, hazelnuts, and peanuts can all be ground coarsely or to a fine meal – similar to flour – for use in desserts. When a recipe calls for ground almonds, the nuts should be ground fine, like flour. Use a blender or the fine blade of a food grinder to pulverise the nuts. Remove skins before grinding. Some skins will come off when nuts are rubbed between your hands. To remove almond skins, boil 5 minutes in water to cover. To toast nuts, spread skinless nuts on a baking tray. Toast in a 180°C/350°F/mark 4 oven until browned as desired. Do not let them burn or they will become bitter and unusable. Grind coarsely or finely, as needed for each recipe.

PANCAKES FOR SPRING ROLLS

sifted strong flour
pinch of salt
peanut oil

Mix 2 parts flour with 1 part water and a pinch of salt to make a thick mixture. Leave to stand for 1 hour. Heat a griddle or frying pan and brush very lightly with peanut oil. Take up a handful of the mixture, which should be quite elastic in consistency, and spread out on the griddle, shaping a pancake approx. 15 cm/6 in diameter. As the mixture cooks (the heat should not be too high) a thin pancake will form which should be carefully peeled off the griddle. Clean the griddle between pancakes with a cloth dipped in oil and repeat the procedure until the required number of pancakes or spring roll cases have been prepared. These spring roll cases can be kept in the refrigerator, covered with a damp cloth.

PANCAKES, MANDARIN (FOR PEKING DUCK)

225 g/8 oz strong flour
sesame seed oil

Sift the flour into a large bowl and make a well in the centre. Pour 5 tablespoons boiling water into the well and work into the flour. Add 6 tablespoons cold water a little at a time and blend into the flour using a wooden spoon until the dough is smooth and soft. Work the dough for a further 5 minutes, cover with a damp cloth and leave for 20 minutes. Roll the dough into a long, cylindrical sausage and cut into 24 pieces. Roll each piece into a small ball between the palms of the hands. Lightly flour the pastry board and rolling pin and roll the balls out into thin, circular pancakes about 12 cm/5 in diameter. Place a frying pan over heat and brush it with sesame seed oil. Add one pancake and cook briefly on both sides; if brown spots appear, the pancake is overcooked. Continue until all the pancakes are cooked. Fold into triangles once they are cooked and wrap in a clean linen cloth, until they are served. This quantity will make 12 servings.

PASTA

The first and most important rule is to cook pasta in plenty of water – at least 1 litre/1¾ pints for every 125 g/4 oz pasta – in a large saucepan. Add 1 dessertspoon of salt to every 1 litre/1¾ pints water. Pour the pasta into the water when it begins to boil. Only filled pasta (ravioli, tortellini, etc.) is added just before the water reaches boiling point to avoid them bursting open. When cooking fresh pasta or lasagna sheets add 1-2 tablespoons of olive oil to the water to prevent the pasta sticking together. Stir the pasta as soon as you pour it into the saucepan, then stir frequently during cooking. For the best results (and evenly cooked pasta) the water should boil neither too vigorously nor too slowly but over a moderate heat. This is particularly important for fresh and filled pasta. Do not cover the saucepan while the pasta is cooking. Drain the pasta when it is *al dente* (tender but still with a little "bite"). Remember that it will continue to cook for a couple of minutes after it is turned into the colander. Filled pasta, gnocchi and freshly made lasagna should be lifted out of the water with a large slotted spoon or ladle as soon as they rise to the surface. Dried pasta and less fragile fresh pasta can be poured straight into the colander. Drain the pasta well if you are serving it straight into individual dishes. Leave a fraction of the cooking water with it if you are dressing it with a sauce in a large serving tureen or if it is returned to the frying pan for a few minutes. If you want to keep and re-use cooked pasta later, drain it when it is *al dente* and submerge in cold water for at least three minutes to stop further cooking. To reheat it, plunge it into boiling water for a couple of minutes, then drain well. The classic way to cook spaghetti is to keep it whole and not break it into shorter lengths. Place the spaghetti in the boiling water and push slowly as the pasta softens until it is completely submerged. Stir.

For perfect success it is important to match the right kind of pasta with the most suitable sauce. As a general rule fresh pasta marries well with lighter, more delicate flavours, such as sauces made with spinach, butter, cream, ham, mushrooms or tomatoes. Dried pasta is better suited to more pronounced flavours and more piquant ingredients, such as garlic, chilli pepper, game, pork and the richer meat sauces.

How to prepare homemade pasta
Fresh pasta
Sift the flour into a mound on a work surface or marble top and make a well in the centre. Pour the whole eggs one at a time (1 egg for every 100 g/3$\frac{1}{2}$ oz flour) into the well, add salt and beat in the eggs with a fork. Continue to beat with a fork until the mixture can be worked by hand. Knead the dough for about 10 minutes by hand. When the dough is smooth and elastic roll out on a floured work surface to the desired thickness.

Fresh spinach pasta
Use 100 g/3$\frac{1}{2}$ oz spinach for every 100 g/3$\frac{1}{2}$ oz flour. Cook the spinach in the minimum of boiling salted water for 5-10 minutes or until tender. Drain well and blend in a blender. Pour into the well in the centre after the beaten eggs. Mix together and knead.

Tagliatelle, fettuccine, tagliolini and pappardelle
Roll out a thin sheet of pasta and cut into strips 25-30 cm/10-12 in wide. Roll each strip over on itself three or four times. Using a very sharp knife cut into smaller strips, 3, 5, 8, 12 mm/$\frac{1}{8}$, $\frac{1}{4}$, $\frac{1}{3}$, $\frac{3}{4}$ in wide depending on whether you are making tagliolini, tagliatelle, fettuccine or pappardelle. Spread the pasta out on a clean cloth to unravel and dry the strips.

Lasagna
To make squares of lasagna, roll out a sheet of pasta and cut into 12 cm/5 in squares. Place the lasagna one at a time in a large saucepan of boiling salted water with 1 tablespoon olive oil to prevent them sticking. Cook for 3-5 minutes; drain when *al dente* and spread out to dry on a clean cloth. Place a layer of lasagna in the bottom of a buttered ovenproof baking pan. Cover with the filling and continue layering with pasta and filling until all the ingredients are used up. Finish with a layer of pasta and place a few flakes of butter on top.

Cannelloni
Proceed as for lasagna as far as cooking. Place a spoonful of filling in the centre of each square of pasta. Roll up into cannelloni. Arrange in a buttered ovenproof baking dish and cover with sauce.

Filled pasta
To make small filled pasta, roll out half the dough into a tin sheet and place small balls of filling on top at regular intervals of about 5 cm/2 in. Brush around the filling with a pastry brush dipped in water or egg white. Cover with the second sheet of pasta. Press firmly round the edges of the filling to seal. Cut out small squares or circles of filled pasta using a pastry wheel or serrated pasta cutters.

PASTRY CREAM

6 egg yolks
250 g/9 oz icing sugar
50 g/2 oz plain flour
$\frac{1}{2}$ litre/1 pint milk
1 tsp vanilla essence or a small piece of lemon peel
15 g/$\frac{1}{2}$ oz butter or margarine

In a medium bowl, beat egg yolks and sugar until pale. While continuing to beat, gradually sift in the flour. Slowly add the milk. Place over a low heat. Add the vanilla or lemon peel. Cook, stirring constantly, until the mixture has thickened to custard consistency (about 15 minutes). Remove from the heat. Discard lemon peel. Melt butter or margarine on the surface of the pastry cream to prevent a skin from forming while it cools. Makes about 60 ml/1 pint.

Variations

Zabaglione pastry cream
Add 2 tablespoons dry Marsala.

Chocolate pastry cream
Add 50 g/2oz grated chocolate or unsweetened cocoa powder.

PESTO SAUCE

25 g/1 oz pine nuts
50 g/2 oz fresh basil leaves
salt
2 cloves garlic
2 tbsp grated Parmesan
200 ml/7 fl oz olive oil

Lightly toast the pine nuts in a hot oven, 200°C/400°F/mark 6. Rinse and dry the basil leaves. Place in a mortar or blender, add salt, garlic and the pine nuts and pound or blend to a paste. Add the cheese gradually. When the paste is smooth, transfer to a bowl and gradually stir in the olive oil using a wooden spoon. Serve with pasta.

PILAF RICE

1 onion
1 tbsp oil
125 g/4 oz butter
350 g/12 oz long-grain rice
salt and pepper
600 ml/1 pint stock

Chop a medium onion finely and sauté very gently in an ovenproof casserole dish in the oil and half the butter until the onion is soft but not brown. Sprinkle in the rice and stir over a high heat for 2 minutes. Season with a little salt and freshly ground pepper. Stir in the hot stock and bring to the boil. Cover the casserole dish and place in a preheated oven at 180°C/350°F/mark 4 for 20-25 minutes. Transfer to a heated serving dish, stir in the remaining butter and serve.

PIPING BAG & DECORATING NOZZLES

When decorating cakes and desserts with whipped cream, icing or buttercream, use a piping bag and an assortment of decorating nozzles. Each nozzle produces a different patterned effect:

Plain nozzle has a small round hole for making drops, blobs, dots and for writing and drawing.
Star or pointed nozzle is used to make stars, rosettes and shells.
Petal nozzle lets you make decorative scrolls, ribbons and delicate flower designs.
Large drop nozzle has a large round hole for making large drops, blobs, dots, writing and drawing.
Flower nozzle is used to make small flowers.
Leaf nozzle makes delicate leaf and flower designs.

PLAIN BOILED RICE

1$\frac{3}{4}$ litres/3 pints water
salt
225 g/8 oz long-grain rice

Bring the water to the boil in a large saucepan; add salt then sprinkle in the rice. Boil for 12-15 minutes or until the rice is just tender. Drain and rinse well. Spread the rice on a clean tea towel on a large baking tray. Place in the oven, preheated to 180°C/350°F/mark 4, for 10 minutes, for the rice to dry.

PRESERVES

Preserve describes several different kinds of products:

Jelly
Clear fruit juice is cooked with sugar to make a gel. Add pectin to juice that does not contain enough natural pectin to gel. Jelly will hold its shape when turned out of a mould.

Jam
Whole or chopped fruit is cooked with sugar. It is soft enough to spread easily.

Preserve
Whole or large pieces of fruit are suspended in a lightly gelled syrup.

Conserve
Conserve is similar to jam with nuts and raisins added. Chutneys may be conserves with onion, peppers and spices added.

Pickles
This refers to vegetables preserved in brine, oil or vinegar and to spicy chutneys made from fruits and vegetables with added garlic, onion, pepper, mustard and vinegar.

PUFF PASTRY

325 g/11 oz flour
1 tsp salt
200 ml/7 fl oz water
150 g/5 oz butter

Sift the flour and salt into a large bowl. Add the water gradually and mix to form a smooth dough. Wrap in a clean cloth and place in the refrigerator for 30 minutes. Shape the butter into a rectangle. Roll out the dough into a 20-cm/8-in square. Place the butter in the middle and fold over the edges of the dough to enclose it. Sprinkle lightly with flour and roll out into a 1-cm/^{1}/$_2$-in rectangle, 50 × 20 cm/ 20 × 8 in. Fold into three, folding the bottom third up and the top third down. Roll out into a rectangle the same size as before. Make a quarter turn and fold the dough in three again. Wrap in waxed paper and place in the refrigerator for 1 hour. Repeat the rolling out and folding operations twice more. Place the dough in the refrigerator for another hour. Remove from the refrigerator 1 hour before the dough is required.

RÉMOULADE SAUCE

400 g/14 oz mayonnaise (*q.v.*)
1 tsp mustard
1 tsp capers
1 tsp gherkins
^{1}/$_2$ tsp chopped basil
^{1}/$_2$ tsp chopped parsley

1 tsp anchovy paste

Mix together the mayonnaise and mustard. Stir well and add the chopped capers, gherkins, basil and parsley. When these ingredients are well blended, stir in the anchovy paste and mix well.

SPONGE CAKE

6 eggs, separated
175 g/6 oz sugar
175 g/6 oz self raising flour, sifted
^{1}/$_4$ tsp vanilla essence

Preheat oven to 170°C/350°F/mark 3. Grease and lightly flour a 20 or 25-cm/8 or 10-in springform tin. In a medium bowl, beat egg yolks with sugar and vanilla until light and fluffy. Beat egg whites until stiff but not dry; fold carefully into egg mixture. Fold in flour. Pour mixture into prepared tin. Bake 25-cm/10-in cake for 40 minutes or 20-cm/8-in cake for 45 minutes or until testing proves the cake cooked. A 20-cm/8-in cake can be split into 3 layers. A 25-cm/10-in cake can be split into 2 layers. Makes 1 (20 or 25-cm/8 or 10-in) cake.

SUGAR, SYRUPS & SWEETS

Test	Description	Temperature
Veil	Sugar is dissolved. Syrup runs from spoon in a sheet.	200-215°F (95-100°C)
Thread	Dropped from a spoon, syrup spins a 5-cm/2-in thread.	230-234°F (110-112°C)
Soft ball Fondant Fudge	Dropped in very cold water, syrup forms a soft ball that flattens slightly when removed from water. When kneaded, it becomes soft and pliable.	234-240°F (112-116°C)
Firm ball	Dropped in very cold water, syrup forms a firm ball that does not flatten.	244-248°F (118-120°C)
Hard ball	Dropped in very cold water, syrup forms a hard ball.	250-266°F (121-130°C)
Soft crack Butterscotch Toffee	Dropped in very cold water, syrup separates into a hard but not brittle thread.	270-290°F (132-143°C)
Hard crack Brittle	Dropped in very cold water, syrup separates into a hard, brittle thread.	300-310°F (149-154°C)
Caramelised sugar	Syrup turns dark golden, but will turn black at 350°F (175°C).	310-338°F (155-170°C)

Caramel is the last stage reached when boiling a sugar syrup. The syrup turns a deep golden brown just before it burns. Caramel is used as a flavouring for desserts, syrups and sauces. Use a small heavy saucepan or frying pan with a flat bottom to caramelise sugar. The heavy saucepan ensures even cooking. In a light pan, it will burn in some spots before it browns in others.

If caramelised sugar is used as a flavouring for custard (as with Crème Caramel, for example) after baking, cool completely, then refrigerate at least 2 hours. This lets the caramel soften and take moisture from the custard. When it is turned out, the caramel syrup will come out with the custard. If turned out immediately after cooking, the caramel is still hard and will remain in the mould.

There are two methods of making caramelised sugar. In one, the sugar is melted and browned. In the other, sugar and water are cooked until browned.

To make the first, stirring carefully, heat 125 g/4 oz sugar over a medium heat until the sugar melts and turns golden brown. As the caramelised sugar cools, it becomes hard, so use immediately. Pour into a mould, tipping to distribute evenly. Or pour boiling water, a little at a time, into the melted, browned sugar to make a syrup. Stir until smooth and all the caramel is dissolved.

Caramel syrup is easily made by boiling 125 g/4 oz granulated sugar and 3 tablespoons water until sugar dissolves. Without stirring, continue boiling until mixture is caramelised. Stirring may cause the syrup to crystallise before it browns. Caramel syrup changes colour fast, so watch it carefully. When lightly browned, it is mild and sweet. The darker it becomes, the richer the caramel flavour – unless it burns. Then it is bitter and not usable. Remove from the heat from time to time to control the cooking. When the colour is deep golden, dip the base of the pan in cold water to stop cooking immediately. Use to drizzle over fruit, or use in recipes calling for caramelised sugar or caramel syrup.

Liqueur sugar syrup
325 g/11 oz sugar
420 ml/1^3/$_4$ pint water
225 ml/8 fl oz liqueur of your choice

In a medium saucepan, combine sugar and water. Stir over a medium heat until sugar dissolves. Stir in liqueur. Makes about 700 ml/1^1/$_4$ pints.

SWEET SHORTCRUST PASTRY

200 g/7 oz plain flour
125 g/4 oz sugar
^{1}/$_2$ tsp salt
125 g/4 oz butter
2 eggs, slightly beaten
1 tsp grated lemon peel or ^{1}/$_8$ tsp vanilla essence

This sweet shortcrust pastry is the basic recipe on which there are several variations. Cocoa powder, ground almonds or hazelnuts can be added. Shortcrust pastry should be prepared as quickly as possible, otherwise it crumbles when rolled out.

In a medium bowl, combine flour, sugar and salt. Make a well in centre. Work in butter. Add eggs and lemon peel or vanilla. Blend all ingredients together until a smooth ball of pastry is formed. Press pastry in bottom and side of tin. Or refrigerate for 30 minutes. Then roll pastry to desired size. Bake at 230°C/450°F/mark 8 for 10 to 12 minutes. Bake tarts or tartlets at 190°C/375°F/mark 5 for 15 to 20 minutes or until golden brown. The quantities given here are sufficient for a 23-cm/9-in flan tin, an 18-cm/7-in pie tin, 9 (9-cm/3$\frac{1}{2}$-in) tarts or 20 tartlets.

TARTAR SAUCE

2 hard-boiled egg yolks
400 ml/14 fl oz oil
salt and pepper
1 tbsp finely chopped chives
1 tbsp mayonnaise
1 tsp vinegar

Finely sieve the egg yolks. Add the oil in a thin stream, stirring constantly. Season with salt and pepper. Add the chives, mayonnaise and vinegar and stir well until the sauce is smooth.

TESTING FOR READINESS

Most desserts are baked for a specific amount of time. However, due to variance in oven temperature, it is always wise to test the product to see if it is cooked. The following are some of the tests that can be carried out:

Custard
Insert a knife in the centre or between the centre and side of the dish. If the knife comes out clean – does not have any custard on it – the custard is cooked. This test is used for individual custards and custard pies.

Bread
Most breads can be tested by tapping the top with your fingertips. If it sounds hollow, the bread is ready. Or remove the bread from the tin or baking tray and tap the bottom with your fingertips. If the loaf sounds hollow, it is cooked.

Quick breads and breads containing nuts or fruit
These are tested by inserting a wooden pick near the centre of the loaf where it will not puncture any fruit or nuts. If it comes out clean and dry, the bread is cooked. If the bottom of the bread is not as browned as you desire, place the loaf directly on the oven rack. Then bake about 5 minutes or to desired brownness.

Cake
Bake minimum time if a range is given before testing. To test most cakes, insert a wooden pick near the centre. If the pick comes out clean and dry, the cake is cooked. If the cake layer is thin, as in a *swiss roll*, press the top with your fingertips. If the surface springs back, the cake is cooked. At any time, if the cake does not seem cooked, return it to the oven for another 5 to 10 minutes. When cooking, the cake should pull away from the side of the pan.

TOMATO SAUCE

400 g/14 oz ripe tomatoes
salt
2 tbsp olive oil
1 tbsp chopped fresh basil

Skin the tomatoes (covering them with boiling water for a few minutes to loosen the skin), remove the seeds and chop the flesh into small pieces. Place in a frying pan with salt to taste and 1 tablespoon olive oil and cook for 6 minutes. Sieve the cooked tomatoes. Pour the sauce back into the frying pan, add the remaining oil and the basil and cook for 1 minute.

VANILLA

When a recipe calls for vanilla, it generally means pure vanilla essence that is obtained from the vanilla plant, a member of the orchid family. Artificial vanilla, which is produced chemically, is widely available but has a slightly bitter taste.

Vanilla sugar
Vanilla sugar is available in supermarkets and speciality stores. But you can easily make your own. In a 600 ml/1 pint jar, combine 325 g/11 oz caster sugar and 1 vanilla bean. Cover tightly. Leave to stand 1 or 2 weeks before using. Shake jar periodically. As the flavoured sugar is used, add more sugar.

YEAST DOUGHS

Almost any dough can be prepared with yeast, from brioche dough to pizza bases to cakes. For desserts and sweet breads, use low-gluten or plain flour. This will give you a more tender product.
Sugar adds flavour and tenderness to bread, helps to brown the crust and gives a delicate texture. It also helps yeast breads to rise faster.
Salt improves the flavour of yeast doughs. If no salt or less than the recommended amount is used, the flavour will be bland and the dough may rise too quickly. Too much salt will hinder the rising of the dough and may spoil the texture of the final result.
Use warm liquid – usually water, milk or fruit juices. If the recipe includes butter or eggs, the amount of liquid required is less.
Always proof yeast. Combine proofed yeast

with other ingredients as the recipe directs. Beat with an electric mixer or by hand. This initial beating shortens kneading time. Kneading is important because it develops the gluten strands, making a fine-textured bread. To knead, place the dough on a lightly floured surface. With lightly floured hands, pick up the dough edge on the side away from you. Fold it toward you. Press down firmly on the dough with the heels of your hands while gently pushing away from you. Turn the dough $\frac{1}{4}$ turn. Again pick up the dough on the side away from you, fold it over and press down firmly while pushing away from you. Repeat this action for about 10 minutes until the dough is smooth and elastic.
After kneading, place the dough in a clean, greased bowl. Cover and let rise in a warm place, free from drafts, until doubled in bulk. This may be done by placing the bowl of dough inside another bowl half-full of warm water or placing the dough in an unheated oven. Place a pan of hot water on the shelf below the dough.
Knock back the dough and shape as directed in the recipe. Again, let rise until doubled in bulk. Bake as directed.
If you are following the batter method, add only enough flour to the yeast mixture to make a stiff batter. Beat well to develop the gluten. Cover and let rise in a warm place, such as over a pan of warm water. Stir down and turn into a prepared tin. Let rise again; bake as directed.

ZABAGLIONE CREAM

3 egg yolks
50 g/2 oz icing sugar
3 tbsp Marsala or white wine
225 ml/8 fl oz whipping cream

In a medium glass bowl, beat egg yolks and sugar until pale. Beat in wine, 1 tablespoon at a time. Place bowl in a bain-marie over a low heat. Beat with a whisk until mixture is light and fluffy. Cool, stirring occasionally. Beat whipping cream until stiff. Carefully fold into cooked mixture. Makes about 700 ml/1$\frac{1}{4}$ pints.

Index

Acknowledgement

The publishers thank the following for kindly supplying photographic material:
Emilio Fabio Simion, Adriano Brusaferri, Giuseppe Losito, Fredi Marcarini,
Shogakukan Publishing Co. Ltd., Tokyo.